women

who do too much

BOOKS BY PATRICIA SPRINKLE

The Remember Box
Carley's Song

MacLaren Yarbrough Mysteries

Who Left That Body in the Rain?
Who Invited the Dead Man?
But Why Shoot the Magistrate?
When Did We Lose Harriet?

Sheila Travis Mysteries

Deadly Secrets on the St. Johns
A Mystery Bred in Buckhead
Death of a Dunwoody Matron
Somebody's Dead in Snellville
Murder on Peachtree Street
Murder in the Charleston Manner
Murder at Markham

Nonfiction

Children Who Do Too Little
Women Home Alone
Women Who Do Too Much

HOW TO STOP DOING IT ALL
AND START ENJOYING YOUR LIFE

women

who do too much

UPDATED EDITION

patricia sprinkle

GRAND RAPIDS, MICHIGAN 49530 USA

We want to hear from you. Please send your comments about this book to us in care of the address below. Thank you.

ZONDERVAN™

Women Who Do Too Much
Copyright © 1992, 2002 by Patricia H. Sprinkle

This title is also available as a Zondervan audio product.
Visit www.zondervan.com/audiopages for more information.

Requests for information should be addressed to:

Zondervan, *Grand Rapids, Michigan 49530*

Library of Congress Cataloging-in-Publication Data

Sprinkle, Patricia Houck.
     Women who do too much : how to stop doing it all and start enjoying your life /
Patricia Sprinkle.
          p. cm.
     Includes bibliographical references.
     ISBN 0-310-24637-7
     1. Christian women — Religious life. 2. Stress (Psychology) — Religious aspects —
Christianity. I. Title.
BV4527 .S665 2002
248.8'43 — dc20   2002007258
                                                                            CIP

Interior design by Nancy Wilson

Printed in the United States of America

---

04 05 06 07 08 /❖ DC/ 10 9 8 7 6 5 4

To Bob,
who sometimes eases my stress
and sometimes adds to it,
but always lives up to his marriage vow
to enable my life's mission as his own

CONTENTS

part three

Weaving Your Dreams into Reality

About the Adventure
of This Book

You are about to start a journey toward a less-stressed life. It will lead you toward lovely vistas of *shalom*—peace, health, wholeness—and distant horizons of things you have always yearned to do. It will also lead you down some thorny paths into your current causes of stress. Getting out may require downright hard work. The good news is that you *can* get out. The better news is that you can make this journey sitting in your favorite reading place with a steaming cup beside you. The even better news is that the path is already mapped by the one who made you. The best news is that you will arrive a lot more rested and hopeful than when you began.

Like any journey, this one requires supplies. You will need a notebook and a pen. Keep a Bible handy. And don't try to make the journey all at once. Pace yourself—a chapter a day or even more slowly if you choose. It is, after all, *your* journey.

There is only one rule for the trip: *Don't avoid the questions*. They are the heart of the journey, the mileposts to mark how far you've come. Without them you are merely flying low over the terrain. Whenever you reach a question, take a few moments to write down the answer in your notebook, then continue reading.

Before we begin, let me tell you a story . . .

Once upon a time there was a woman who was very busy for God. She worked twenty hours a week as a director of

Christian education. She wrote articles for Christian magazines and was part of a weekly prayer and Bible study group.
Because she knew God cares about hurting people, she chaired
her city's literacy council, served on the board of a home for
unwed mothers, chaired its publicity committee, and went to
the home one evening a week to befriend the girls. She knew
God also cared about justice and hunger, so she served on
three hunger committees, volunteered in a local food pantry,
led workshops about hunger, edited newsletters for two
hunger relief organizations, and helped coordinate a Christian
organization devoted to political advocacy on behalf of the
hungry.

Did I mention that her husband directed a city-wide ministry, and she sometimes spoke to groups on its behalf?

Every day she was busy for God. Wasn't she happy and
fulfilled?

Actually she was frustrated and overwhelmed. No matter
how much she got done in a day, she fell into bed every night
knowing she had left important tasks undone. She woke up
every morning knowing she had far too much to do.

Does that sound like your story? It is my own.

Back then, my days were filled from morning until night
with good works for God. Except, of course, for hours I
squeezed out to indulge in binge reading. I'd feel guilty about
those hours, but couldn't seem to help myself. A fast reader, I'd
skim through seven books in two days, leaving everything else
undone. I'd make excuses to people I was letting down. I'd beg
my husband not to let me read so much, then sneak out of bed
in the middle of the night and go to the front bathroom to read
so he couldn't see the light. Finally one night I took our church
youth group to a seminar on alcohol abuse. When the leader

handed out a list of symptoms of addiction, I saw that I had an addiction of my own.

A harmless one? No addiction is harmless. It gets between us and God and us and other people. Those of you who have been similarly addicted to alcohol, sex, drugs, television, the Internet, overeating, or compulsive shopping know what I mean. The world's demands overwhelm us, so we convince ourselves that only we can meet our need for "fun" in our lives. What we do isn't really fun—we know that. But because it was once fun, we keep doing it over and over, hoping this time will be better.

At the time, I thought my life would always be a seesaw of overwhelming good things to do, followed by a binge of self-indulgence. I truly believed I was God's servant doing God's work with occasional pauses "to take care of myself."

One night our prayer group came to our house for dinner—twenty people. Afterward, my husband introduced the Lord's Supper with the truth that it is sin to participate in communion if we are out of charity with a brother or sister. Looking around that room, I wasn't in charity with any of them. They were in my house, and I yearned to be alone.

"I'll be back," I muttered to the woman next to me and headed out the door.

We were living in St. Petersburg then, so I headed for my favorite walk by Tampa Bay. The moon was full over the water and the breeze brushed my cheeks, but I scarcely noticed. I was so angry! Since the waterfront was empty, I could rage aloud.

"Where are the love, joy, and peace you promised if I served you?" I demanded of the Creator of the evening sky. "The only fruit of the Spirit I've got is long-suffering."

In the silence that followed, I heard the voice of God.

I have often heard God's wisdom spoken through Scripture or the words of a friend. I've known the direction of God through doors that unexpectedly opened or closed. I've felt the nudging of God in my own conscience. But that night I heard a voice. It felt as if every pore of my body was an ear, and an enormous voice filled the universe with one startling word: "Rest."

"What do you mean 'rest'?" I demanded. "I can't rest. I've got too much to do."

"Rest."

"I can't rest," I insisted. "Just look at tomorrow and what I have to do." I started to list my schedule, which started with a 7:30 meeting and ended with an 11:00 P.M. deadline.

The voice came a third time. "Rest."

By that time tears of frustration were streaming down my cheeks, but I felt a twinge of hope. If my Boss thought I needed to rest, maybe it could happen. I pictured myself in a nice bed with clean white sheets and people to wait on me while I had a well-earned nervous breakdown.

God spoke this time in an idea. "Give up the home for unwed mothers." I knew that was God, because the idea would never have occurred to me. I'd taken on that job because two of my best friends were on the board, and they had assured me the board desperately needed my publicity and writing skills. How could it get along without me? I'd barely wondered, when I had an unflattering thought. "I don't need you there. You are doing that for your glory, not mine."

Ouch!

"What about the literacy council?" I asked.

"Serve your term and get off."

"What about hunger?" I figured I was on a roll. Pretty soon I'd be reading books all day.

Instead, that voice filled the universe one last time. "Emphasize it."

That was all I heard that evening, except for the peaceful rustle of wind in the palms. I returned nervously to my house, wondering how I'd tell my two friends (who were both in the prayer group) that I was resigning from their board.

As soon as I entered my house, I discovered something: If we open ourselves to the will of God, God does not work in one person's life without simultaneously working in others' lives to accomplish the same purpose. The group was praying when I got there, and to my astonishment I heard one of my friends from the board saying, "Lord, Patti is real stressed right now. If there's anything I can do to help her, please show me what it is."

Before I could make my presence known, the other friend added, "And Lord, we pray for your will to be done in all our lives." God had already prepared them for what I was going to say.

Now, if this were really a "once upon a time" story, I'd tell you that since then, my life has been free of stress and I've blossomed into somebody who does the will of God "happily ever after."

But this is real life. That night by Tampa Bay was, for me, only the beginning of a journey of discovery. I've spent a good bit of my life since then trying to determine what it means to listen for the will of God before I make decisions, big or small. What it means to seek to do only those things God wants me to do, without running ahead and trying to anticipate what that might be. What Scripture has to say about how God intends us to live as servants and heirs of the Kingdom.

At the same time I have had and raised two sons, discovered and fulfilled my dream of writing mysteries and other novels, and tried in each place we have moved to find some way to do something concrete to help the poor.

This book is partly about my journey. But because my journey is not your journey, the book is based not just on my own experience, but on the experience and wisdom of fourteen women I interviewed for the first edition and on the experience of women I've met since then at seminars and retreats in the United States, Canada, and Venezuela. Their stories pepper these chapters. Perhaps you will recognize your own.

So grab a pen and a notebook, curl up in your favorite reading place, and let the journey begin.

part one

This Isn't Working!

> *"For surely I know the plans I have for you,"*
> *says the Lord, "plans for your welfare and not*
> *for harm, to give you a future with hope."*
> —Jeremiah 29:11 NRSV

chapter one

Women in Frantic Search of Shalom

*A*re you always busy, yet never seem to get everything done?

Do you wake up frustrated and even angry, because you have more to do today than you can possibly accomplish?

Do you go to bed feeling guilty, knowing how much you have left undone?

Do you lie awake at night planning tomorrow, because you won't have time to think once you hit the ground running?

You don't have to live there; it is a matter of choice. In fact, it's the wrong choice. God has a better idea. It is found in the Hebrew word *shalom*, which we will talk about throughout this book. *Shalom* means all those things we yearn for: peace, wholeness, prosperity, success, well-being, health, and salvation.

This book is going to explain how we get ourselves into a place where we are too busy and overwhelmed to experience *shalom*, and how we can get out of our current ruts to live lives of grace, joy, and even leisure.

We will begin by considering where stress comes from and what remedies there are to deal with it. We will then explore how our dreams and yearnings—even those we have allowed to become buried beneath the muck of our busy lives—may in fact be God's dreams and yearnings for us. We will look at how to focus on what is important for us and pare down the rest.

At the end of the book I give a few tips for getting through busy days with far less stress. But don't turn to the back right away. If you do, you will just learn to be more and more efficient at doing what you don't want to do anyway. How do I know? I've been there.

Let's begin this journey with an incredible promise that makes sense of our lives.

LIFE IS A TAPESTRY

> "For I know the plans I have for you," declares the Lord, "plans to prosper you and not to harm you, plans to give you hope and a future."
>
> —Jeremiah 29:11

This promise is a lot richer in Hebrew than in English. The Hebrew noun that is usually translated "plan" actually

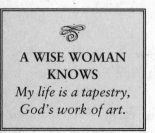

A WISE WOMAN KNOWS
My life is a tapestry, God's work of art.

means an artistic design, and the verb is not "to have" but "to weave." In fact, this particular form is both a verb stem of "to weave" and the noun "weaver." Hebrew, a practical language, often omits unnecessary words, so the first part of the verse can be literally translated, "For I know the design which I, the Weaver, ... for you." Just as Jeremiah elsewhere describes God as a potter working us like clay, here Jeremiah presents God as the Divine Weaver, creating a pattern for our lives. Think of Navajo rugs, medieval tapestries, Persian carpets. That is what God intends our lives to be like—intricate, rich in meaning, and lovely.

Furthermore, this verse in Hebrew also takes pains to describe exactly what kind of design God intends to weave for us. God's design is *not* that we will be run ragged all day and exhausted at night. Rather, the word the NIV translates "prosperity" and the NRSV "welfare" is actually *shalom!* Everything that shalom means—health, success, well-being, peace, salvation, prosperity—is part of God's artistic design for us.

Finally, the design God is weaving for our lives includes a future with hope and expectation. Doesn't that sound great?

 How does my current life compare with God's design? *

EXPECT A FEW RAPIDS

Don't think, however, that this book is about How to Spend the Rest of My Life Lazing by a Stream Eating Bonbons. This book is about finding God's plan for your life. Sometimes God's plan is a calm and placid stream and sometimes we have to shoot the rapids. Or, to return to our original metaphor, sometimes our life tapestry is quiet and pastel, sometimes it is complicated and vivid. The Divine Weaver plans so that each new part of the pattern enriches the whole.

---

*These questions provide time to pause and consider your life in the light of what has been said. They are the most important part of the book, so please don't skip them. Keep a notebook and pen handy.

As I write this chapter, I am in a particularly busy part of my pattern. Ten days after my deadline for completing this book, a moving van will take our furniture to Atlanta, where my husband will write grant proposals for nonprofit ministry organizations. Moving company representatives, exterminators, plumbers, electricians, and air conditioner repairmen march through the house to interrupt my work. Boxes—empty and half-filled—sit in every room. Friends call wanting one more lunch together. Committees call wanting one more meeting. Our realtor calls about problems with the contract on our new house. We have to buy a refrigerator and carpet before we can move in. Yesterday an editor called to say she needs the title for my next mystery, so her art department can begin work on the cover. A special friend I haven't seen in years just came to town to sing in an upcoming opera. And last month my mother-in-law's doctor called and said she can no longer live alone. We moved her in with us, and as soon as I send our furniture on its way, she and I have to detour by Tallahassee to choose the furniture she wants to keep so we can close her house.

She jokes that she has come to live at Grand Sprinkle Station. We certainly aren't a placid stream right now. But does that mean my life has slithered away from God's plan? Not at all. God is just giving me a new pop quiz on Surviving the Storms of Life. It has questions like,

> Can you trust me with the little details in all this confusion?
> Can you trust that all of this is part of my plan for you right now, and I will make everything that is important fall together without your needing to worry or becoming over-stressed and exhausted?
> Do you believe so completely that I am in charge of your life that you can take time even in the busyness to spend

quality time with others, notice the glint of sunlight on leaves, listen to a bird outside your window, or enjoy one last glorious swim in your pool without thinking of things you ought to be doing instead?

Will you remember to thank me for little mercies that make these days easier?

Let me give you some examples of God's little mercies. One day I discovered I needed to get a paper notarized. I wasn't sure how that would fit into the schedule, but I am intentionally not getting stressed these days over minor details. That very evening we had a committee meeting at the house and when one of the committee members saw the paper lying on my countertop, she said, "I'm a notary. Why don't I take that back to the office and fax it for you?" Isn't that amazing? I've known her four years and never knew she was a notary.

When I brought to God the problem of trying to think of a mystery title while writing this book, I remembered twelve friends who love to read mysteries and are great with words. A quick e-mail got them racking their brains for a title for that book while I wrote this one. The title someone else chose is far better than any I would have thought of.

Now I have handed over to God the question of two stray cats we've been feeding on the front porch, a mama cat and a kitten. Will God find a home for them before we leave? Stay tuned.

God's plan for our lives is not that all the circumstances will be peaceful or even pleasant.

God's plan *is* that we will experience *shalom* in each of them and know that our future has hope.

So why isn't that the way life really is?

Practice the Presence of God

One way to look at our lives is as a tapestry. Brother Lawrence, a seventeenth-century lay brother, suggested another metaphor. Although he spent his lifetime humbly working in a monastery kitchen, he learned and taught others to do what he called "practicing the presence of God." His writings have been published in many editions in small devotional books by the same name. He tells how he prayed:

> Sometimes I think of myself as a block of stone before a sculptor, ready to be sculpted into a statue. Presenting myself thus before God, I beg Him to form His perfect image in my soul and make me entirely like Himself.*

TRY THIS EXERCISE

Close your eyes and picture yourself before the throne of God. You are a stone and God is a carver. Ask the carver to form you in God's perfect image. Spend a few minutes trying to picture what the Divine Carver may be going to do with you and your life.

---

*Brother Lawrence of the Resurrection, *The Practice of the Presence of God*, John J. Delaney, translator, Foreword by Henri Nouwen (New York: Doubleday, 1977), 70.

chapter two

"I Do It All for You, Dear"

What causes most of your stress?

When I ask that question in seminars, people invariably laugh and say, "Other people."

Some elaborate:

"Kids."

"My husband."

"Parents."

"My boss."

"Students."

I don't know about you, but sometimes I fantasize about running away to a cottage somewhere in the woods or by a beach with just enough modern conveniences to make life comfortable and no other people to make life complicated. I have no idea whether that life would actually be simpler or not, but I do know that one primary cause of stress for most women is other people. Many of us are nurturers by nature. We want other people in our lives. But if we do too much for parents, children, spouses, coworkers, friends, and members of our congregations, we discover that their demands and needs threaten to overwhelm us.

One woman told me, "When my husband died and left me with four small children, I felt like I was being nibbled to death by ducks. Some days it seemed like every one of them needed something every single minute. One evening I put them to bed, wrote a farewell note to them, got in my car, and headed west. I firmly intended to call the police from the next town saying the children had been abandoned, and I planned to never come back. Then I pictured their little faces and I knew I could not desert them. But I could not bear to go back either because I knew they were going to consume me. I stopped by the side of the road and wept and wept. I cried until I felt God saying, 'Claire, I will not abandon you. You do not have to do this alone. But you don't have to meet all their needs, either. Those children still have a heavenly parent. Trust me to meet some of their needs.'" She gave me a rueful smile. "That didn't mean it all got easy, but at least it got easier."

Knowing how busy some women are about the needs of others, I am surprised Jesus didn't expand the parable of the three stewards in Matthew 25 to include a "stewardess" who comes back with the master's original talents in her pocket to explain, "I was going to invest them on Monday, but that afternoon my boss had an emergency and needed me to work late. Tuesday little Mikey got an upset stomach at school and I had to leave work early to take him to the doctor. Wednesday my best friend's marriage fell apart and I spent the evening with her. Thursday after work my mother needed me to take her shopping. Friday I went straight from work to church to plan next summer's Vacation Bible School. I know you told me to use the time you were gone to invest your talents, but all those other people *needed* me." Wouldn't you think Jesus would have awarded her the whole pot for selfless behavior?

Unfortunately, he did not include this scenario in his story, so we must conclude that all of us will one day be rewarded by the Master on the basis of how well we invested the talents we were given, not on the basis of how well we met everybody else's needs.

Later in this book we will begin to consider ways to identify our talents and determine what it is God has created each of us to do. First, however, we need to develop a repertoire of techniques we can use to deal with other people who will, if we let them, devour our lives.

WHY WE WRAP OUR LIVES IN OTHER PEOPLE'S NEEDS

In order to stop doing something that has become a habit, we need to figure out why we do it. Here are some of the reasons women devote their entire lives to other people. Read through them and consider which of them—or what else—may motivate you to do too much for other people.

A WISE WOMAN KNOWS
If you don't decide how to spend your life other people will decide for you.

We Get Our Theology Backwards

> "Teacher, which is the greatest commandment in the Law?"
>
> Jesus replied, "'Love the Lord your God with all your heart and with all your soul and with all your mind.' This is the first and greatest commandment. And the second is like it: 'Love your neighbor as yourself.'"
>
> —Matthew 22:36–39

If we live as we are created to live, our primary love is toward God, then we equally love ourselves and other people. What do we try to do instead? We get those two great commandments backwards. We put other people up where God is supposed to be, and spend most of our time trying to show how much we love them. We love God with whatever time and energy we have left. And we think we are being religious by always putting ourselves last. In high school I was taught that JOY stands for Jesus, Others, and Yourself. It is a cute and catchy acronym, but it's not Judeo-Christian theology. A triangle is a better picture. God is at the apex and we and other people are at the two base corners.

What does it mean to love God more than you love anybody else? Think back to a time when you were in love. What was that like? Women in workshops have given these answers:

- You make sure you spend as much time with the other person as you can.
- You do things that please the other person.
- You learn to like things he likes and you introduce him to things that you particularly like.
- You think about the other person all the time.
- You study him to learn all you can about him; he fascinates you.
- Just thinking about him makes you happy, talking with him makes you happier, and being with him makes you happiest of all.
- You neglect other people to spend time with him.

While loving and being in love are not always synonymous, those definitions do describe the way many of us relate to various others in our lives. We devote our days to them, eat chicken legs when we'd rather have breasts because they like the breast, get up at night to throw in a load of wash so they'll have clothes to wear in the morning, and neglect ourselves and God because we have too much to do for them. So consider . . .

How well do those definitions of love describe my relationship with God?

How well do they describe the way I treat myself?

We cannot love either ourselves or others appropriately until God is the first love in our life. We cannot love others *appropriately* until we love them "as"—both "in the way that" and "at the same time that"—we love ourselves.

Some people love themselves too much, of course. Generally they are the ones who go around claiming, "I just can't love myself," but since they talk about themselves incessantly, think about themselves exclusively, and insist that all conditions of life make them comfortable, the rest of us know they love themselves. It is a sick kind of love that puts themselves where God is supposed to be, but because it is sick, it won't do any good to point out that they love themselves. Perhaps the best thing we can do for them is to say, "Don't worry about *trying* to love yourself. Love God. Spend time with God. Study about God. Sit in silence before God. Once you love God, you will learn how to love yourself, because God loves you."

The rest of us—those of us who do more for everybody else than we do for either God or ourselves—can learn from Beth, who said, "I used to think my stress came from raising four children in the midst of ministry. My husband is a seminary professor and we often have students and groups in our home. Keeping schedules sorted out kept me hopping. But recently I have come to see that most of my stress comes from deep within me. The Hebrew word that we translate 'iniquity' means 'twisted places.' God has showed me that one of my own twisted places was being a people pleaser. For years I felt torn by trying to balance husband, kids, our extended family, and friends. Now I'm learning that all I have to do is please the Lord Jesus. All I have to be concerned about is discovering what God wants me to do, and doing just that. Then I don't have to worry when I'm with one person that I ought to be somewhere else, or that someone will be unhappy about what I'm doing."

>
>
> **A WISE WOMAN KNOWS**
> *Almost anything you do is going to make somebody unhappy.*

I have a sneaking suspicion that for some of us, we do so much for other people because we fear that what we do for others now is *less* than what we'd be asked to do if we actually asked what God would have us do. That's when we need to remember what God promises in Jeremiah 29:11. God's plan is for our welfare, not our harm, to give us a future with *hope*.

 How can I better express that I love God with all my heart, soul, mind, and strength?

 How can I express love for myself in ways I already express love to others?

We Pity Others' Circumstances

Ann's daughters developed juvenile diabetes when they were very young. She said, "I had low expectations of help from my children and was willing to spend money and most of my time taxiing them to dance classes, art lessons, cheerleading, horseback riding, piano lessons, Brownie Scouts, and choir because I thought I could make up in some degree for the shots, food restrictions, and blood and urine tests that were such a part of their lives. I excused my children from helping me to compensate them for living in a less-than-perfect world. In doing so, I failed to teach them skills they would need as grownups in the world."

We Try to Keep Our Own Lives Under Control

Betty said, "For me, it was an issue of control. I tried to control my husband, my six children, and others within the sphere of my environment, because I thought I needed to control them in order to control my own life. I couldn't even nap because I'd think, 'I have to be awake in case that serviceman comes. Could the kids really tell him what to do?' God finally had to remind me that I was not called on to be God, who sleeps neither day nor night. I had to lay down my compulsion to control."

We Like Things Done Our Way

I am astonished whenever a woman boasts, "I am a perfectionist," as if that were something to be proud of. What a perfectionist really means is, "I like things done my way." If you don't believe that, put two perfectionists on the same committee.

A perfectionist mother may not teach her children household skills they will need later, because she can't stand having the house "messy" while her children learn various tasks. A perfectionist professional does far more than her share of the work because she doesn't trust her coworkers to do it "right." A perfectionist wife doesn't share household responsibilities with her husband because the husband does things differently. Many of my own early marriage conflicts arose because Bob wasn't raised by my mother.

However, life is too short and precious for any of us to go through it doing everything for other people because we believe our way to do anything is the only way. God has different designs for different lives. We sin if we try to shape everybody else in our own image. Besides, think how much free time we acquire by letting other people do some things their way.

We Can Do Things Faster

Those of us accustomed from early childhood to taking charge and getting things done have developed the knack of getting two or three things done at once. Multitasking is the current buzzword for that. Multitaskers can simultaneously bathe one child, plan a homeroom end-of-the-year party on the phone, and oversee another child's homework. Multitaskers can cook a meal in under an hour while finishing a chapter on the computer and listening to a friend pour out her heart. How do I know? Because for years I was proud to be one. Every Christmas when I read in Luke 2 that the shepherds "made haste" to go to the manger, I knew I'd probably have tried to fit in a few errands on the way there and back.

Multitaskers can plan a Sunday school lesson, run a committee meeting, organize an event, or clean a house faster than anybody we know. Therefore, we do a lot of things other people could be doing, "to save time." The problem is, the time we save isn't our own. The more we do, the more others let us do, until we move so fast our lives resemble a merry-go-round at high speed.

Pride is at the root of multitaskers' lives, just as it is at the root of perfectionists' lives. We don't love God or other people, we love speed and efficiency. One of the struggles for me, as for other multitaskers, is to remember that the goal of life is to be effective, not merely efficient. Part of loving other people as I love myself means to let others do tasks at their own pace.

 Who am I doing too much for because
- *I pity their circumstances?*
- *I am trying to keep my own life under control?*
- *I want things done my way, not theirs?*
- *I can do things faster?*

WAYS TO LIVE WITH OTHERS WITHOUT WEARING OURSELVES OUT

Obviously we are going to continue to live with love and to serve other people. But serving them too thoroughly is not good for either us or them. Here are three steps that can relieve some of the stress of serving others.

Just Say No

This sounds easy, but it's not. Saying no involves admitting we are not indispensable, that others can do some things for themselves. It involves convincing ourselves that what we feel called to do is as important as what someone else wants us to do. It may even result in something that is scary for some of us: free time. Below are a few rules for when to say no.

- When what you are being asked to do is something you know you don't do well.

A WISE WOMAN KNOWS
Procrastination on your part does not constitute an emergency on my part.

- When what you are being asked to do conflicts with something you feel is more important.
- When another's procrastination has resulted in a crisis for them.
- When what you are asked to do is not in line with the goals you have prayerfully set for this season of your life (we'll get to that in later chapters).

- When you are being told "Nobody else will do this if you don't." If God wants it done, God will call somebody else to do it; if she says no, then it is not your problem.

To whom do I need to say no in order to have more time for what God is calling me to be and do?

Teach Them to Care for Themselves

This applies to children*, spouses, and coworkers. If we are doing something for others they could do for themselves with a little training, spending time teaching them is a wise investment of our time. We not only relieve our own stress, we give them the satisfaction of learning a new skill and moving

---

*See my companion book to this one, *Children Who Do Too Little* (Zondervan, 1996).

toward self-reliance. One woman put it, "I have taught my husband to run a house because I don't want him having to stop on the way home from my funeral to get himself a new wife."

> **?** *What skills do I need to teach to whom to enable them to be more self-sufficient and to reduce my own stress?*

Negotiate and Reciprocate

This is a mind-set that acknowledges that each of us has something to give and each of us has something we need. When our boys were younger and I was driving them to baseball practice and games, we negotiated so that each child returned some of my time by doing one extra chore a week.

While a couple was in the midst of building their retirement home, they came to one of my workshops. The wife told me all about the house and added, "I want Italian tiles in the kitchen, but he thinks they are too expensive." Later, the husband explained to the group how he hoped to have a dog, but added, "She doesn't want the mess a dog could bring into the house." One of the other participants, who had grasped the negotiate/reciprocate principle, asked the wife, "How badly do you want those tiles? A dog's worth?" The wife looked at her husband for a long minute, then nodded. "I'll give you the dog for the tiles." They sealed the bargain that afternoon and ended two stresses in their marriage.

Raye was running a business out of her home, but her elderly mother was bored and kept calling to ask Raye to drive her around their old neighborhood and take her to lunch. Finally Raye sat down with her mother and worked out a deal. Every morning the mother comes to Raye's house to answer the phone and perform simple office tasks like preparing a mailing or entering names into a database. In exchange, Raye stops working every Wednesday at noon and she and her mother go out to lunch, drive around, perhaps even take in a movie or go shopping. Raye reports there's been an unexpected bonus: her mother fixes lunch.

> **?** *How might negotiation and reciprocation with someone reduce my own stress?*

"IF YOU WOULD ONLY . . ."

There's one last reason a lot of us wear ourselves out doing too much for somebody else. We do too much for some people because we don't think they can run their own lives.

After Gene's husband asked her for a divorce, he developed a debilitating illness with a long recovery period. He asked her to stay with him until he was on his feet again. When she agreed she said, "My priest spoke of my 'fire-bucket behavior' and pointed out that I didn't let others suffer the consequences of their own behavior because I truly didn't think they could take care of themselves."

That reminds me of the sailors in the story of Jonah, who threw their whole cargo and personal possessions overboard trying to save Jonah from the consequences of his behavior. How often do we rescue people and thereby come between them and the lessons God wants to teach them, lessons that might actually turn their lives around?

When a family member or a close friend seems helpless to run his or her life, or consistently makes what look to us like dumb or even dangerous decisions, we want so badly to advise and even to make good decisions for them. We yearn to help them avoid painful consequences of bad decisions. We tie ourselves in knots trying to figure out how we can change the person. Surely, if we try hard enough, we can fix his or her life.

The truth is, no amount of effort on our part is going to change someone else's basic nature. God puts certain traits and character into people before they are born. Some are dashers and some are dancers—and each group has a tendency to drive the other crazy. Some seem to be inherently neat and others thrive on varying degrees of disorder. One mother who raised six children marveled at how different they all were, and described her two youngest sons, who shared a room. "One made his side of the bed neatly every morning. The other stored extra motorcycle parts on his side when he wasn't sleeping in it." Both grew up into responsible, although very different, adults.

In addition to what we are born with, each of us develops various habits as we grow up. We become people who habitually make good decisions or who generally make bad ones. We become either a truth-teller or someone who slides around the edges of truth. We develop preferences about things like how many people we like to be around and how much noise we can stand in our environment.

No matter how much you and I try, we cannot change another person's character. Of course, God can. However, increased effort (nagging) on our part seldom teaches them to make better decisions or get out of situations we don't like. Sometimes the best thing we can do is get out of the way and let natural consequences teach the hard lessons they need to learn.

At the same time, we have to accept that they may have no desire whatsoever to become who we want them to be, or to do what we want them to do. We cannot force a child to stop using drugs or alcohol, make a sister leave her abusive husband, change the negative attitude of one of our parents toward the other, or make a rose out of an ornery coworker determined to stay a thorn.

That doesn't mean we have to live with all the stress the relationship causes. While we cannot change them, we can change ourselves, and how we relate to them. We can change

- how much of our lives they are permitted to fill with chaos.
- how we enable or fail to enable their current behavior by lying to cover up for them or providing money when they are "fresh out."
- how many of our own resources—money, patience, lodging, hours of listening—we give them.
- how much access they have to our lives.

We can also decide how loving we will be, when we will offer tough love, and when we will be compassionate and kind.

Let me give you a little hope here, though. Sometimes when we want to change another person, it is helpful to remember the apostles Peter and Paul. Their friends and relations must have wanted many times to curb Peter's impetuosity and blunt tongue or soft-pedal Paul's zealous bigotry. Yet it was precisely those traits that God transformed into Peter's bold sermons and courage and Paul's missionary zeal.

A WISE WOMAN KNOWS
I can never change someone else. All I can change is myself.

Just think: The very traits you are trying to change in somebody may be what God will eventually use in their lives to build up the kingdom! Don't get in the way.

 Is there someone I've been wearing myself out trying to change? Since I cannot change that person, what will I do instead to reduce my own stress in this relationship?

REMEMBER . . .

Other people belong in our lives, but they should not consume them. In order to love God first and love others as we love ourselves—and avoid loving others more than we love ourselves or God—we have to let go of some of what we do for them, teach them to do for themselves, and believe they can succeed on their own. We may have to give up our own need to control them or have things done our way and at our pace. The result can be more time to fulfill our own callings and dreams. The result can even be easier, more pleasant relationships with other people.

chapter three

Put Your Adrenaline Where It Matters

Gloria, a psychological counselor, described a whole year of non-stop situations that required enormous energy on her part: "My ninety-year-old mother was hospitalized ten times. Finally it was necessary for her to come live with us. That meant selling our house and finding one that could accommodate us all. The day after we moved, we were in an accident that left me with whiplash injuries. Since Mother needed nursing care in our home, I had to find someone to care for her while I was at work. Our younger son graduated from college that spring. We planned to take our first trip to Europe to recuperate from the months we'd had, but the day we got back from our son's graduation, Mother died. We held her funeral the day before we left for our vacation. Six weeks after we returned, my husband retired."

Do you think Gloria was overwhelmed that year? Definitely. But Gloria's year of stress illustrates the fact that while a great deal of our stress may be related to other people, sometimes it is not people themselves who cause our stress, but situations we face together. Gloria's mother wasn't obnoxious, she was old. Her son wasn't rebellious, he was graduating from college. Her husband wasn't unpleasant, he just reached retirement age. Those were not "people" stresses, but "situation" stresses—which can be equally hard to live with.

A "people" stress is caused by character, personality, or relationship in which people make demands or have expectations of us that are greater than we can comfortably meet. A situation stress is caused by circumstances.

Every situation exists somewhere on this continuum:

Situations we   **Situations we**
can change _____ **cannot change**

Most of us know the Serenity Prayer:

Lord, grant me the serenity to accept the things I
    cannot change,
Courage to change the things I can,
And the wisdom to know the difference.

Put another way, there are a couple of important rules to reducing stressful situations. First, don't sweat the stuff you can't do anything about. Second, do everything you can to reduce the stress in the rest.

SITUATIONS WE CANNOT CHANGE

Recently a young attorney told me bluntly, "I don't believe there are situations we cannot change. I have never encountered anything I couldn't do *something* about."

She was both right and wrong. There is generally something we can do to reduce our personal stress in any situation. However, each of us eventually faces some situations we cannot change or control, and which have the potential to greatly increase our own stress. Things like

- traffic jams and other people's accidents, which slow down our own journeys;
- stock market fluctuations, or increased taxes, which reduce our income and worth;
- times of change that bring with them unexpected stresses;
- terrorists who bomb buildings and snatch weeks from a nation's life;
- friends whose lives are out of control;
- family members who get themselves in hot water by their own bad decisions;
- votes that don't go our way;
- aging and deterioration of appliances, cars, and bodies—our own and those of people we love;
- job loss, chronic illness, and fatal disease.

An hour and a half before we were supposed to close on our house in Miami, we got a call from our attorney's office. "The buyer's attorney has uncovered five open building permits on the property, dating from before you bought the house. The work was never inspected. Even though it has nothing to do with you, the buyer can't legally close this deal until something is done about them."

That was a perfect example of something we could do nothing about. Miami building inspectors are so busy it can take ages to get inspections completed. Our stress levels rose, however, as we thought about the new house we were supposed to buy in two days in Georgia with the proceeds from this one and the carpet layer who was coming the night we closed on the new house to get down the carpet before the furniture arrived the next morning. I have seldom felt so helpless.

Remedy 1: Hand the Situation Over to God

Doreen has a "God bag," a large paper bag with God's name on it. She told me, "Whenever I come up against something I simply cannot do anything about, I write it down and put it in the bag. 'This is yours, God,' I say. 'I can't wait to see how you deal with it.' Periodically I take the slips out and read them. It is amazing what has happened in some of those situations once I gave them to God."

Prayer certainly improves any situation that we cannot change.

 Which causes of my current stress are situations about which I truly can do nothing? Take a minute to turn them over to God.

Remedy 2: Do What You Can to Minimize Your Own Stress

Shirley was living in Key West with four children when her husband, a Naval officer serving in Vietnam, wrote that he had already divorced her and married somebody else. That was a situation about which Shirley could do absolutely nothing. "What I could do was return to my parents' town, find work to support myself and the children, and build a new life. But talk about stress! If I hadn't come to the Lord at that time, I'd have lost my mind."

Donna's husband had two malignant brain tumors, five years apart, before he was forty. Radiation on the second left him seriously mentally impaired. Eventually, he began to have seizures and psychotic episodes that frightened and endangered their children. Neither Donna nor her husband could change the illness. He could not even change himself. Donna had to come to terms with that. All she could do was make decisions about the extent to which she would let that illness control their family. After much prayer and painful discussion with friends and family, she decided to put him into an assisted living facility. That decision did not change their situation, it only made the stress more manageable.

In our situation regarding the open building permits, people scrambled for twenty-four hours to see what could be done and still found no easy solutions. Eventually the lawyers agreed we could close the deal, but only if we left a sizeable amount of money in escrow in Miami to pay all costs until the permits are closed. Bob and I have chosen not to fret over things we cannot do to the new house until that matter is completely settled.

 What steps can I take to relieve my own stress in situations I cannot change?

SITUATIONS WE CAN CHANGE — IF WE WILL

Having admitted that there are some situations we cannot change, we have to also admit that in most situations, we can do more than we have done.

We once invited to dinner a guest whom we wanted to get to know. Bob went for groceries, but got delayed. I set the table, arranged the flowers, baked the sweet potatoes, started the vegetables, and fumed. Our important guest arrived before the ham I had planned to bake for his dinner.

When I greeted him with profuse apologies, he said heartily and with no concern whatsoever, "I passed a chicken place just down the road. Why don't I run back and get a bucket of chicken to put with what you've got?" He arrived home just as my sheepish husband pulled into the driveway. When I apologized once more, our new friend said something I have never forgotten: "The problem is generally not the problem, but what you do with the problem."

The astonishing thing is how often we would rather complain about a situation or endure enormous stress than sit down and figure out something to do about it.

My husband used to watch soap operas, a form of entertainment based entirely on stress. If a character doesn't have some type of stress in his or her life, off the show they go. My husband's rationale for watching them was that as a pastor he counseled so many people who lived by what he called "soap opera theology":

- I can't do a thing about this mess—I can't even move away and leave it behind.
- If I am tempted to do something wrong, I'm likely to do it.
- If I make a mistake in my life, it will haunt me forever.

How many of us live by that kind of theology, as well?

Christian theology assures us that God will make a way in all situations, God will make sure we are never tempted beyond our ability to withstand it, and God forgives our sins and restores us to abundant life. Remember, God has a design of *shalom* for our life tapestry. Since stress will be a part of it, our task is to seek paths to *shalom* through the stress. How can we decide how best to relieve the stress of given situations?

Step 1: Analyze the Situation for Alternatives

Seeing our situation down in black and white can help us understand why we are overwhelmed and burnt out. Prayerfully analyzing the situation can help us come up with creative solutions. Here are two methods that can help you analyze your own situation.

The List Method of Analysis

Mary Jane was facing a non-stop week. "The week hasn't started and I'm already tired," she admitted. So she sat down and listed everything she had to do, by category.

Mary Jane's Week

House: clean, cook, grocery shop (buy and prepare food for party next Saturday), hold party, clean up from party

Office: plan conference for next month, write newsletter, edit annual report

Church: plan vacation Bible school, practice and sing in choir

Family: weekly orthodontist appointment for Sue, drive Timmy to baseball 3x week, Timmy's game Saturday a.m., drive Frank to airport early Thursday, pick up Saturday noon, take Mother to dentist Wednesday

Note: It is critical when making a list like this to put on it *everything* you are doing. Leaving out something like "cook," which takes hours each week, won't give a true picture of why you are burnt out. A quick look at Mary Jane's list shows there was not one single thing there to refresh or bring pleasure to Mary Jane herself, with the possible exception of the party. "I am beginning to dread it," she discovered. "It sounded like a good idea when we decided to do it, but by this time it's just one more thing to do."

Mary Jane also saw by writing down the list that she was doing a lot for other people without expecting them to do anything in return.

That particular week, her biggest stress items were three major projects at work and the upcoming party. While in another week the big stresses in her family might be Sue's ballet recital, Timmy's all-star game, or Frank's big presentation at work, this was a week when she needed the family to rally around her. She needed to ask for help.

Mary Jane saw several things she could ask others to do to relieve her stress: (1) ask Frank to leave a car at the airport for two days; (2) ask Timmy and Sue to cook one meal each or do some extra cleaning in return for being driven to the orthodontist and baseball practice; (3) ask her mother to have the family over to supper once while Frank was out of town. She also decided it wasn't a good year for her to help plan and run Vacation Bible School.

Finally, she asked herself some "emergency mode" questions: "Would our budget permit hiring somebody to clean before and/or after this party?" She decided what to cut out in order to make that possible. "How can I make the party simpler?" She decided to use prepared food trays and quick dishes from wholesale grocery stores. "Could somebody at work help me with the newsletter and planning the conference?" She recruited assistants, and also concluded, "This sure looks like a week for a lot of take-out food and canned soup suppers."

As Mary Jane considered her past year, though, she saw that her job frequently caused stress for the whole family. When any one area of life produces constant stress for ourselves or our family, it's time to evaluate that particular area in its entirety to decide whether it is worth the stress or whether less stressful solutions could be found. In Mary Jane's case, she went to her boss with an analysis of when she had had to work overtime and weekends during the past year, and requested assistance in coming months for times when the workload would be heaviest.

The Life Picture Method of Analysis

I personally prefer, when overstressed, to draw a life picture. Later in the book I will confess how I failed to take my own advice at one point in my life, and got myself into a situation where I was gasping for breath for one whole semester while I finished a master's degree. Here's the life picture I drew that awful spring to help me figure out how to survive:

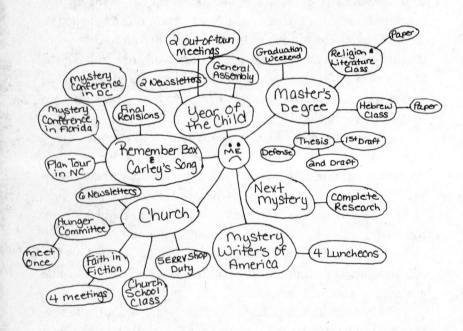

Those large balloons radiating out from Me in the center represent each area of my life at the time. The smaller balloons around those balloons were specific situations or demands that were producing stress. Anybody with sense who looked at that picture could see I had bitten off far more than I was going to be able to chew. The memory of that semester still makes me shudder.

However, just drawing a picture like this is a form of do-it-yourself art therapy that relieves some stress. For one thing, we begin to see that we are not crazy to feel overwhelmed. We feel overwhelmed because we *are*. We also begin to see that we have given equal weight to too many things when we can only handle a few major ones at once. Seeing it all surrounding us on paper can help us decide which balloons need to lose some of their air for the time being and which of them may even be let go entirely to focus on what is more significant.

Step 2: Look for Initial Small Steps

Years ago we moved into a house that was under renovation. As we lived for weeks amid Sheetrock dust, lumber scraps, and odd pieces of plywood, I became more and more overwhelmed by the chaos. One day as I sat hopeless, considering the mess, our kitten walked daintily into the room, sat down, and looked at her dusty paws in distaste. Then she gave me a withering look that plainly said, "You could at least sweep."

I fetched a broom and swept. The room looked so much better, I decided to carry out scraps of lumber. I moved the plywood out of view and realized I could throw a bedspread over a stack of unpacked boxes to make a colorful corner. As I completed one task, I saw another. First that room, then gradually the house began to assume a semblance of calm and order.

Most situations can be alleviated if we remember the wisdom of that kitten: "You could at least sweep." Making a start on solving a problem stimulates us to think of additional solutions.

Ann described how that worked in her life. "My mother did all the housework, laundry, and cooking, and I grew up and followed her model. But I added being a college professor and taking an active role at church. When our two daughters both developed juvenile diabetes at a young age, that required numerous urine tests, blood tests, and insulin shots every day. Dealing with the house, students, and two children with a chronic, time-consuming illness was a recipe that spelled stress."

In order to avoid utter burnout, she looked at her situation and made significant changes. "I intentionally gave up ironing and bought only permanent press clothes. I hired a maid every other week for the primary cleaning. Instead of cooking a different meal every night, I made quantities of stews, soups, or roasts and served them several times in a week. My husband and I both taught at the community college, so we arranged our schedules so that one of us was home with the children while the other was teaching. That had an obvious payoff in terms of the relationship of our girls with their father. The evenings I taught, he was the one who gave baths, read stories, and monitored their diabetes—so much so that when she was five, our older daughter made a plaque at school that said, 'My daddy reads me stories when Mommy doesn't come home at night.'

"The change that made the most difference was a swap arrangement we made with my in-laws. They were retired, loved Florida, and no longer liked to cook. John and I needed experienced help with the children so we could both teach. His parents added a suite of rooms to our house and came down for each school year to provide childcare, and I cooked for all of us. It sounded like more stress to cook for six and worry about getting everybody to the table at once, but I discovered they preferred to eat while watching television. So I'd take supper in for them to eat when they wanted it, and the rest of us sat down whenever I was ready. How I lived was not how my mother lived. I adapted to our situation so I could enjoy being a mother and a professor at the same time. I think we all need to identify our own expectations and refuse to be pressured beyond them. We need to say, 'What I can manage is *this*.'"

In my awful semester, I decided I needed to give up teaching Sunday school and ask the participants to teach it themselves. I spoke to my professor of Religion and Literature and arranged to write my paper for that class on how mystery novels are used to teach religion—which permitted me to relax with a couple

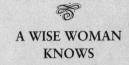

A WISE WOMAN KNOWS
What I can do is what I can do, and what I can do is enough.

of mysteries and write on something I already knew a bit about. I informed all committees and groups I was part of that I would not be attending any meetings for the rest of the semester. I canceled business trips out of town and arranged for someone else to cover for me. I asked for help wherever I could find it. That semester was still one of the hardest times of my life, but I managed to eliminate unnecessary stress and focus on what mattered at the time.

Sections two and three of this book will discuss in detail how to determine what is most significant, how to set goals to move toward accomplishing that, and how to pare down the amount of time we give to insignificant things. Remember though that the best ordered life will have times of major stress. Seeking small ways to reduce stress often leads to additional steps we can take.

A Chinese proverb tells us that a journey of a thousand miles begins with one small step. So does our journey toward *shalom*.

As I consider situations currently causing stress in my life, what changes could I make that would reduce my stress and make life more manageable? Will I make them?

chapter four

Wise Up Before You Burn Out

 wo other major reasons why we get overwhelmed and burnt out are because

- we operate in high gear for too long a stretch and/or
- we do what is inappropriate for us.

OPERATING AT HIGH GEAR FOR TOO LONG

Although so far I've spoken of stress as if it were a bad thing, stress itself is a God-given gift. Humans are made so that when we meet a situation that requires more energy than we normally have, our bodies produce extra hormones and blood sugars to accomplish extraordinary tasks. That's how we get through the last mile of a marathon, the last pushes of childbirth, the annual report, and the pots and pans after Thanksgiving dinner.

When our older son was four, he investigated the underside of a queen-sized hide-a-bed sofa we had turned on one end while our floors were being sanded. The couch was top-heavy, and the whole thing fell, pinning most of him underneath. As soon as I heard his shrieks, I dashed from the kitchen, lifted the couch, and moved it half-way across the room.

Bob and our pediatrician, who was also a friend and neighbor, left me with our infant son while they took Barnabas to the hospital with, thank God, nothing worse than a broken leg. After I put the baby to bed, I thought I might as well push the couch across the rest of the room to its usual place.

I can't push that couch. I certainly can't pick it up. It takes two strong men to lift it.

Yet, when it threatened my son's life, I handled it like it was made of cardboard. My body performed as it was created to perform under stress.

The reason we feel drained after stress, however, is because we literally are. When sugar and hormones have surged to provide extra energy, they recede. That's why we feel as drained after happy experiences such as making a successful professional presentation or spending a day at the beach as we do after a harried day at work or cleaning out the garage.

Our bodies are created to surge with plenty of energy to meet challenges, then to collapse and recover. Expecting our bodies to perform under stress for hours and hours, or for day after day, is like constantly driving a car at racing speed, or running a blender on high all the time. Constant stress wears anything out.

Remedy for Operating At High Gear

Since operating at high gear for too long at a stretch burns us out, we need to pace ourselves so that times of great exertion and challenge are followed by time to relax and recuperate. I once worked simultaneously for two organizations, one three days a week and one two. One was an all-woman staff, the other employed mostly men and a few women. The all-women staff met twice a week, first thing in the morning, for devotions and to share what was going on in our lives. Afterwards, we had donuts and coffee. We took coffee breaks together most mornings, had a monthly covered-dish luncheon to celebrate birthdays and milestones. If a staff member had an out-of-town trip or worked over a weekend, she was urged to take compensatory days to recover. Sometimes when we were going to a particularly interesting place, our executive suggested we stay for a day or two afterwards to rest and sightsee.

The "mostly men" staff scheduled devotions once a week, but many staff were too busy to come. Our only luncheons were sack-lunch working sessions. We hurried back to our desks from out-of-town trips to catch up on work we'd missed while away. I don't ever remember a compensatory day or celebrating a birthday or a personal milestone as a group.

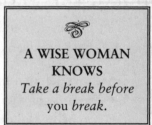

A WISE WOMAN KNOWS
Take a break before you break.

Oddly enough, the staffs accomplished the same amounts of work. Furthermore, most of my women coworkers lived well past their eighties and some into their nineties, while many of the men died before they were seventy and some before they were sixty.

This is not a woman/man difference, of course. I have known women executives who drove their staffs very hard and men executives who insisted the staff balance work and family lives.

The point is, both men and women—and every family unit—need periods of down time to recover from stress. After times of enormous stress we need longer to recover. Human bodies cannot be driven all the time.

Gail, mother of four and an active volunteer in many organizations, said, "A growing place for me is to accept that if a day is too full, I've filled it too full. I've accepted too much to do. I'm having to realize that other people and outside forces don't cause my stress, I do. So, with God's help, I can control it."

> *When is my next period of high stress that is likely to exhaust me and/or our family? What sorts of things could I (we) do during that time and immediately afterwards that could help me (or us) rest and recuperate?*

DOING THE WRONG THINGS

As I've conducted workshops and spoken with many people, I have discovered that far too many people are doing . . .

- too much of what we don't want to do,
- too little of what we do want to do,
- too many things we don't do well, and
- the same old things when it is past time for a change.

Doing Too Much of What We Don't Want to Do

If each of us could start fresh with a clean slate, how much of what we are doing now would we continue to do? Many women, I find, spend a majority of their time doing things they do not enjoy. Things we don't enjoy tend to drain us and take the joy out of life. So why do we do so many of them? Often, because

- somebody else told us we ought to,
- we think we can do what we're doing better than anyone else, or
- somebody persuaded us that if we don't do an important task, nobody else will.

In the introduction I told how two friends who served on a certain board told me they badly needed my writing skills to help with public relations because nobody else on the board had that particular skill. When I finally realized I was not on that board because God intended for me to be there, I gathered my courage and resigned. That very day another board member said, "I know somebody who runs a public relations firm in town who has been wanting to be on this board, but we haven't had a vacancy." That person turned out to do a far better job than I ever had.

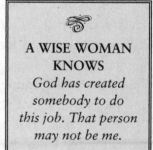

A WISE WOMAN KNOWS
God has created somebody to do this job. That person may not be me.

Doing Too Little of What We Want to Do

I had never identified "doing too little of what you want to do" as a major stress factor in women's lives until one particular workshop. When I mentioned that we need to listen to our dreams, I saw tears start down one woman's cheeks. I made a mental note to speak with her privately, never imagining how God would use that conversation to show me a major truth.

"My problem isn't that I am doing too much," she explained. "I saw as you were talking that my problem is I'm not doing enough of what I *want* to do. I'm trained as an artist.

I majored in art in college and planned to paint. But my family persuaded me to also get my teaching certificate, and as soon as I graduated, I got a good job teaching kindergarten. I've done that for seven years and I'm a good teacher, but I haven't touched a paintbrush in ages. This morning I realized that most of my stress comes from wanting so badly to paint and not doing it."

Several days later I saw her again, and she glowed. "Sunday afternoon, I'd planned to go to my classroom and cut out construction paper dinosaurs to begin a new unit Monday. Instead, I stretched a long roll of paper around the room and painted dinosaur scenes for hours. You should have seen the children's eyes light up when they came in Monday morning. And I know now that whatever else I do, I must paint."

On my plane ride home, I thought back to that time in my own life when I was doing far too much. I had already identified what I thought was the cause of my stress: running at high gear doing things I wasn't designed or called by God to do. It had never occurred to me that at the very same time, I was *not* doing something I wanted to do: write mysteries.

Years before, looking over our budget, my husband had asked, "Why don't you write a murder mystery to pay for the ones you buy?" Immediately, I knew the story I wanted to tell, and began *Murder at Markham*. I discovered that for me, writing a mystery is as much fun as reading one. But when friends heard I was writing a mystery, many were aghast. Some Christian friends informed me I would do far better to write inspirational materials. One even claimed that mysteries are demonic. Folks who worked with me on the issue of hunger were equally chagrined. "People are starving to death in the world and you are writing *mysteries?*"

Between them, they shamed me into shelving my mystery manuscript in a far corner of my closet. For years I wrote only inspirational materials and for hunger education publications, but I still went to bed each night with a mystery novel because they help me relax.

Finally one night I found myself sobbing beside a lake, "God, I wish I could write a mystery."

When I confessed that to my husband, he asked, "What would you need to change in order to write one?"

"For one thing, since it's set in Chicago in February, I'd need to go back there during the winter so I could remember how it smells, looks, and feels." Given that we lived in Florida and our budget was stretched, such a trip seemed impossible. I forgot that conversation and went back to my regular activities.

God did not forget. The following February, when it was 72 degrees in St. Petersburg, we got a call from Chicago, where they were fast approaching a record 192 inches of snow. A church there wondered if Bob would like to interview to become their pastor. Our immediate reaction was, "Heavens, no!" But we agreed to fly up and meet the congregation.

Not until after we had accepted the call and moved to Chicago the following summer did I connect that move with my sobbed prayer by the lake. The God who gives exceedingly more than we can ask or think—and sometimes more than we might want—arranged for me to spend the next five Februaries in Chicago, giving me enough time to draft *Murder at Markham* and get a good start on a second mystery.

Since then, I have realized that writing mysteries and other fiction is my call from God. Saying yes to that calling in spite of what others might think released God to open doors in amazing ways. It has also been a major means of reducing stress and providing energy in my life.

Think for a moment about women who focus most of their time and attention on things they love. Aren't they women who smile and laugh a lot, women who have lots of energy, who have time to spend an hour or two with a friend without guilt that they ought to be doing something else? Those women are cooperating with the design God is weaving in their lives, functioning as God intends us all to function: energized by and enjoying what we do and living with enthusiasm, laughter, and leisure.

In chapter 7 we will look at ways to test whether our own dreams may be God's vision for our life, in spite of what others may think. We will also discuss how to begin to claim neglected dreams and develop buried gifts. Meanwhile, think about the following questions.

> **?** *Are there things I am currently doing that I truly do not enjoy and wish I could stop doing? Why am I doing each of them? Is that sufficient reason to continue?*

> **?** *Is there something I yearn to do that I have either stopped doing or have never tried?*

Doing Things We Don't Do Well

Maxine, a medical lab technician, described a time when she was asked to teach a nursing lab course. "Talk about stress! I'm not a teacher, and I didn't like it at all. That taught me to concentrate on what I do best."

All of us have some things we do well and some we don't. Accepting our limitations can reduce our stress.

Linda planned all her life to be a missionary and spent four years in Africa as a Bible translator, but she was frustrated and unhappy. Too much of her time was spent taking care of her own daily needs or in solitude, translating. She missed her family and yearned to work directly with people. She returned home for a year to think things over, and decided to go to physical therapy school. While working as a therapist, she met and married a man equally committed to international ministry. They purchased a large house where international students now live with them and their two young daughters. They also hold Bible studies where Christian students from many countries meet and get to know one another. Instead of going into the world, Linda discovered that in God's design for her life, the world comes to her.

 Are there things I am doing right now that I know I do not do well?

Doing the Same Old Thing When It Is Time for a Change

Have you ever noticed how much easier it is to take on a job or start a new group than it is to give up a job or terminate a group? As a child I used to go watch my grandfather's mules grind sorghum cane to make molasses. Around and around those mules went, turning the grindstone. Eventually they wore a rut into the earth, and when they were released after a day's work, it was still easier for them to walk in a circle than a straight line. Every time I hear the word "rut," I think of those mules.

We aren't mules, but how often do we keep going in the same wearying circles because it is easier than making a change?

Maybe we remember a time when that job was fresh, that commitment new and exciting. Or we really don't enjoy what we are doing, but we believe the group or cause is worthwhile, and fear nobody else will do it if we don't. How many times have we heard this cry: "If nobody joins our group, it will die." As if that were a bad thing.

In John 12:24, Jesus speaks not just of his own death, but of many other facets of life. "Unless a kernel of wheat falls to the ground and dies, it remains only a single seed. But if it dies, it produces many seeds."

For several years, Enid was involved in a weekly prayer and sharing group. Initially it was a great group, but after a while its members began to sink into a mire of always discussing the same issues and making the same prayer requests. Enid began to dread Thursday evenings and wished she dared quit, but felt the others counted on her. Finally she took a deep breath and admitted to the group one week, "I have set some goals for my life, and I want to use Thursday evenings to work on them." Her honesty forced the rest of the group to look at their own purposes for being there. They decided, reluctantly, to disband. However, several members called later to thank Enid, expressing their relief. One member put it succinctly, "Our group lived out its natural life span and we kept it on life support systems. You were the only one with the courage to pull the plug."

Since that group has disbanded, its members have spread out into their congregation and now head up several new ministries and study groups. Ecclesiastes 3:2 tells us there is a time to be born and a time to die, but when it comes to giving up things we've done a long time, do we believe that?

Now let's look at something else that causes a lot of stress for some of us.

What am I currently doing that I am tired of doing and would like to stop doing in order to do something else?

chapter five

Heavy Spirits Are Hard to Carry

*J*oanne loves her children, her church, her home. She hates her ex-husband. Talking with Joanne is fun until Walt's name comes up. Somehow, it always does. Then her face grows tense, her voice harsh. You want to move away in embarrassment as she recounts details of how he betrayed her. Joanne went to her doctor with migraine headaches and to a counselor with problems in parenting her children, but even after the doctor helped her headaches and her children went away to college, Joanne remains bone-tired and depressed. She can't seem to complete tasks or make long-term plans for her life.

Linda is a top-notch teacher and a choir member who leads a weekly Bible study. However, if you are with Linda for any length of time, you hear about her mother: a domineering, unloving woman who never gave her children respect, attention, or freedom to fail. Linda dreads holidays when she must go home to visit her mother, and always returns exhausted. She also has a lot of stress in her professional life. According to Linda, women in authority over her never give her the respect or advancement she deserves.

Sarah is lonely. She wishes she could get close to others, but she has been disappointed so often she no longer even tries to make new friends. One former friend shared her secrets. Another got married the spring she promised to go with Sarah to Europe. A third—male—seemed headed for marriage, then veered off. Sarah wasn't really surprised. Her own father wasn't reliable, either. But she wonders sometimes why people can't be trusted. What is the matter with everybody?

These women all have a common problem. They all carry a sackful of blame and its related cousins: anger, resentment, judgment, and desire for revenge. These "rocks of offense" are extremely heavy, for over the years they tend to attract to themselves *every* wrong committed against us.

Other women carry a sackful of guilt and its related cousins: shame and a sense of unworthiness. Guilt, like blame, attracts to itself every mistake or sin we commit.

When we carry rocks of offense very long, our spirit's sack can become heavy. Blame, guilt, and their heavy cousins lower our spirits, increase our stress levels, and color *all* our relationships. Before we can become who we were created to be, we must get rid of rocks of offense—and every one of us has a load of each; our sacks are just different sizes.

> Let us throw off everything that hinders and the sin that so easily entangles, and let us run with perseverance the race marked out for us.
>
> —Hebrews 12:16

GETTING RID OF BLAME

There is a simple way to get rid of blame: forgive. But while forgiving someone is simple, it is also hard. It requires a deliberate, intentional act of will on our part.

We know, of course, that we should—even must—forgive. In the Lord's Prayer, Jesus taught that God forgives us *as*—both "while" and "in the manner that"—we forgive others. However, most of the time we feel justified in holding on to our grievances. If the other person has done something wrong and not asked our forgiveness, why should we give it? Even if they have asked for forgiveness and then repeated the offense, aren't we forgiving too easily? Frederick Buechner says, "Of the Seven Deadly Sins, anger is possibly the most fun. To lick your wounds, to smack your lips over grievances long past … is a feast fit for a king."*

We also live in a society that tends to focus on understanding rather than forgiving. We are offered a myriad of reasons why people hurt one another: an abusive spouse probably came from an abusive home, a coworker who snaps at another may be under a lot of stress at home, a parent who never attends music recitals or ball games could be overworked. The implication is, if we can understand why someone hurts us, we will be able to excuse them for doing it.

The problem is, excusing is not forgiving. Excusing no more heals a spirit's genuine wounds and scars than your understanding how I gave you the flu and excusing me for doing it cures your flu. So even after we have excused somebody because we understand why they did what they did to hurt us, our spirit wounds remain. We find ourselves still getting angry in similar situations, avoiding the person who has hurt us, or carrying a heavy rock of blame that permeates the rest of our lives.

---

*Frederick Buechner, *Wishful Thinking* (New York: Harper & Row, 1973), 2.

We don't understand that unforgiveness is an acid that destroys its container. We don't notice how blame slows down everything else we do, wears out our bodies, and consumes our days. We don't realize that getting rid of blame is the first step toward relieving our stress and getting our lives back.

Unforgiveness in our spirit may even manifest itself in illness of the body. Years ago an organization I worked for decided to restructure, and in the process inflicted a great deal of pain on some of my closest friends. I became very angry, consumed by what I told myself was a "passion for righteousness." I found myself unable to sleep at night, and when I did, my dreams were angry. My nose started to run—not a drip, but a river. Then one Sunday I heard a sermon focused on Christ who brings peace and forgiveness. A question began to nag me: "Have you forgiven those people?"

Initially, I thought, "Of course I haven't forgiven them. They didn't hurt me, they hurt others." But I was so relentlessly hounded by that question that finally I sat down and listed every person I was angry with and every offense I could remember. I went down the list and forgave them. I also confessed my own nastiness toward them, and asked God's forgiveness for that. My nose stopped running! I learned then what harm unforgiveness can inflict on our bodies as well as our spirits, and what a barrier unforgiveness can be to getting on with the rest of our life. I also saw the power of forgiveness to heal.

Mary's family discovered how forgiveness can heal after they found that their new house was built over five springs that kept their basement damp and their back yard soggy. They asked the builder to fix them, but he had not seen the springs when the house was being built, so he refused. They took him to court and lost. For months they fumed and raged. Every conversation eventually got around to how angry they were at the builder and their situation. Then one Sunday the whole family seemed lighter, happier. They invited the church to a party in their back yard the following month. We found a volleyball net where they'd had soggy ground and a nice den in what had been a wet basement. What happened? "We decided to forgive the builder and borrow money to have the springs capped," Mary told us. "Forgiving the builder was the hardest. Capping the springs was a piece of cake after that."

Catherine Marshall discovered one more reason to forgive: "I've found this forgiveness business a key to getting prayers answered."* Forgiveness not only frees us and the one we have forgiven, it also seems to free up God to relate to us both again. Marshall came to understand this truth through David du Plessis, a South African pastor, who gave her insights into Matthew 18:18: "Whatever you bind on earth will be bound in heaven, and whatever you loose on earth will be loosed in heaven."

"I found out," du Plessis told her, "[that verse] means that by hanging on to my judgment of another, I can bind him to the very conditions I'd like to see changed."†

Impressed by that insight, Marshall and her husband spent their prayer time for several mornings listing on legal pads anything they could remember that anyone else had done to cause them pain, hurt, or anger. Then they prayed to forgive and release each person from their own judgment. They not

---

*Catherine Marshall, *Something More* (New York: McGraw-Hill, 1974), 38.

†Ibid. All of chapter 3 in *Something More* deals with the topic of forgiveness.

only found themselves released from bitter feelings, they also began to see changes within those persons.

Not all forgiveness is just between us and God. Sometimes we must go to a person who has wronged us to seek reconciliation. That involves not only forgiving them, but also asking their forgiveness for carrying grudges, holding onto anger, perhaps talking about them with other persons, or responding to them with less than love. This type of forgiveness may take time, but can result in both improved relationships and spiritual growth for both persons involved.

A WISE WOMAN KNOWS
You should always forgive your enemies. It will please some and bewilder the rest.*

Jesus illustrated the highest forgiveness when he spoke from the cross, "Father, forgive them, for they do not know what they are doing" (Luke 23:34). His forgiveness was based on the great truth that it is not *our* forgiveness that ultimately matters to another, but God's. It also acknowledged that none of us truly knows the depth of the bruises we inflict on others. This type of forgiveness not only releases another from our judgment; it also asks God to release the person for all eternity from blame in the matter.

To Get Rid of Blame

- Ask God to remind you of people who have wounded you and events that have left you with wounds and scars—things that still cause you pain, anger, or humiliation to remember. Jot down a word or two to remind

---

*This is a paraphrase of Mark Twain. What he actually said was, "Always do right. It will gratify some people and astonish the rest."

you of each incident you want to forgive. The first few times you do this, you may want to use a page for each five-year segment of your life or one page for each important person.

- Go down the list and say aloud, "God, I forgive [name] for [incident]." Speaking aloud is important. God doesn't need to hear you say those words, but you do. At the end, say, "God, I turn [name] over to you and release my blame."

- For each incident, confess your own sin, as well: anger, resentment, jealousy, keeping something secret when it should have been revealed, revealing what should have been secret, bearing a grudge, or whatever the Spirit shows you. Ask God to forgive your sin in that situation.

- Destroy the list. Burning it can be a symbolic gesture. So can tearing it into tiny shreds.

- Repeat these steps often to keep your spiritual sack empty of blame toward others.

GETTING RID OF GUILT

As hard as it is to forgive others, it is harder to confess our own sins. It is even hard for most of us to name them. We live in a society that talks about "false guilt" and seldom admits the real thing. I once went to traffic court to pay a speeding fine. And yes, I had been speeding.

I found a line stretching out the door and down the walk. After waiting half an hour, I discovered I was in the Not Guilty line. "Where's the line to pay?" I asked.

"If you were going to plead guilty, you'd just go up to the desk and pay," I was told, "but nobody does that." Several lawyers offered to get me off. Instead of waiting over an hour and expecting a lie to be believed, I confessed, paid the fine, and left ten minutes later with my conscience clear. I couldn't help picturing a similar scene one day in the throne room of heaven.

We women are guilt experts. Guilt poisons our lives in many ways. We feel guilty that we aren't doing enough. We feel guilty we are doing too much. We feel guilty we aren't giving our family enough attention. We feel guilty that we are smothering them. We feel guilty we aren't spending enough time in prayer. We feel guilty we aren't working, and we feel guilty that we are. One woman admitted wryly, "Sometimes I feel guilty for feeling so guilty."

On the other hand, in the middle of all that guilt, how often do we stop to take stock of what we have actually done in a day to wound others? Words we spoke in haste or anger. Promises we did not keep. Acts of unkindness toward friends and strangers—in our homes, our community, and on the highway.

The church is often guilty of suppressing confession. How many congregations include a true confession of personal sin in their weekly worship service and leave enough silence to search our souls?

A WISE WOMAN KNOWS
A clear conscience is often the sign of a bad memory.

Yet, carrying around a load of unconfessed sin increases our stress. We avoid certain people or situations. We pretend nothing really happened. We act extra nice and hope the person we wronged will "excuse" us. All that time, a dark ugly place is festering inside us.

Fortunately, the Holy Spirit stands ready to help us uncover those festering places and clean them out. As a starting place, we can use the confessions of earlier generations.

John Wesley's Oxford Club met weekly to ask one another questions like: Do I confidentially pass on to another what was told me in confidence? Can I be trusted? Is there anybody whom I fear, dislike, disown, criticize, hold a resentment toward, or disregard? If so, what am I doing about it?

In his classic devotional guide, *My Utmost for His Highest,* Oswald Chambers asks these questions: Have you renounced "the hidden things of dishonesty"—the things that your sense of honor will not allow to come to the light? Are you paying your debts from God's standpoint?

John Baillie's *Diary of Private Prayer* contains this confession:

> A heart hardened with vindictive passions;
> An unruly tongue;
> A fretful disposition;
> An unwillingness to bear the burdens of others;
> An undue willingness to let others bear my
> burdens;...*

Did any of those prick you as you read them? That is one way the Holy Spirit nudges us to confess our sins.

To Get Rid of Guilt
- Thank God for forgiving your sins and giving you the desire to follow Christ. State your intention to renounce your sins and ask the Holy Spirit to reveal past actions you need to repent of. The first few times you may want to focus on a particular relationship or one period of your life.

---

*John Baillie, *A Dairy of Private Prayer* (London: Oxford University Press, 1965), 119.

- Jot down things that come to mind. Don't get side-tracked in reliving old memories. Focus your mind on listening to God.

- Repent aloud for each sin. Do not explain or try to justify your actions; simply say, "God, please forgive me for [specific sin]." Pause to accept God's forgiveness before confessing the next sin.

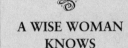

A WISE WOMAN KNOWS
Sometimes the reason we feel guilty is because we are.

Ask God to use your confession to bless the person you may have sinned against.

- If you feel a need to confess certain sins to a person you have wronged, star those items and plan to schedule a time with the person.

- A long-range strategy and even counseling may be needed for extremely damaged relationships. Plan ways to rebuild those.

- Destroy the paper. Again, burning can be an important symbol that your sins are forgiven.

 As I listen, who does the Holy Spirit remind me that I need to forgive? What does the Holy Spirit remind me of that I need to confess, so that I may be forgiven and get on with my life?

LIVING HAPPIER EVER AFTER

Sometimes the hardest part about forgiving or confessing is believing we really did it. In the pain of new offenses, old memories come back. We think, "I must not really have forgiven that person," or, "Maybe God forgave me, but I can't forgive myself." The favorite words of the Father of Lies are "You didn't really..." Sometimes our task is simply to respond, "I did too."

Remember, it is not necessary for us to *feel* as if we have confessed or forgiven, it is enough that we have done so. If you keep suspecting you haven't really forgiven someone, forgive them again. But it is a matter of Christian discipline to claim that when we have forgiven another, God has ratified that and it is done. When we have confessed our sin in repentance, God forgives it.

It is also a matter of Christian discipline to realize that we cannot forgive ourselves; only God and others can forgive us.

If we confess our sins, God is faithful and just and will forgive us our sins and purify us from all unrighteousness.

—1 John 1:9

If you try to forgive or confess and are still haunted by fears that your forgiveness or confession was not "real," find a counselor or pastor who will help you heal those memories. The end result, getting rid of barriers that produce additional stress in your life, is worth any time it takes.

chapter six

One Slingshot and Five Smooth Stones

As I live my own life and listen to others speak about theirs, I find that in addition to an unhealthy load of sin and guilt, most of us have one pesky issue that crops up again and again to increase our stress. For Rachel it was a fear of poverty. She grew up painfully poor. Even after she and her husband earned comfortable incomes, she worried that one day their money would all be gone. "I could tell myself I trusted God with my whole life," she admits, "but I used to get the shivers whenever I saw a homeless woman. I was terrified that would one day be me." When she eventually conquered that fear, she found herself worrying that her grown children would not earn enough to live on, or would live beyond their means. "I still struggle not to nag them about how they spend their money," she says, "but I can look back and measure my spiritual growth by how well I am dealing with that one issue."

Terry, in her fifties, has wrestled for years with being single. "When I was younger, I wanted romance. Later I began to long for companionship. Now I yearn for security—someone who will be there when I get old and infirm. My desires have looked different in various stages of my life, but the central issue has been the same."

My own issue is trying to balance several claims on my time at once. In college I wrestled with how much time to spend on studies and how much on social life. As a single young adult I struggled with how much of myself to give to work, how much to give to church commitments, and how much to social life. As I have aged, I have continually juggled the priorities of marriage, our children, my calling to write, and commitments in church and the community. This book is one fruit of that quest.

Even as I write this chapter, I am showing our house to sell it and adjusting to having my husband's mother live with us. All through the day I have to ask, "Which is more important right this minute, my deadline, meeting her needs, or agreeing to show the house right now?"

For years, the fact that I had to struggle with that same old issue seemed inconsistent with my Christian faith. If I were truly following God, would I have to wrestle with several important demands on my time? Why couldn't I get permanent victory in that area? Rachel asked a similar question: "If I truly trust God, then why do I fear poverty?" Terry asked, "I believe God is sufficient for all my needs, so why do I keep yearning for somebody to share my life with?"

PHILISTINES: A GIFT OF GOD FOR THE PEOPLE OF GOD

For years I flippantly called my struggle with several competing priorities my "Philistine issue," simply because it was always there. Remember the Philistines? They are most prominent in the stories of Samson and Delilah and David and Goliath, but the Philistines are woven throughout Israel's history. Abraham lived with the Philistines for many years. Isaac prospered among the Philistines at Gerar. When Israel returned to the Promised Land, several judges including Samson struggled against Philistine armies and the insidious influence of Philistine culture and religion on the people of Israel. Saul, Israel's first king, warred with the Philistines for several years before the giant Goliath appeared. David killed Goliath, but fought the Philistines well into his reign. In the time of King Ahaz several generations later, Judah battled Philistines.

What does that have to do with you and me?

Years after I'd begun to call time management my "Philistine issue," I discovered what Scripture says about the Philistines and other nations of Canaan in Judges 3:1–2: "These are the nations the Lord left to test all those Israelites who had not experienced any of the wars in Canaan (he did this only to teach warfare to [those] who had not had previous battle experience)."

Do you realize what that means? God *gave* Israel the Philistines to teach them how to do battle. Is it possible that our own Philistine issues are a theme woven throughout our life tapestry by a wise Creator to test our ability to trust and follow God? Like Rachel said, we can measure our spiritual growth by how well we have learned to deal with our particular issue.

 What one issue have I wrestled with for years and years, yet it keeps coming back in different forms?

 Am I wrestling better now than I was five years ago? Ten years ago? In what ways? What have I learned about myself and about God in the process?

HELP! MY PHILISTINE IS A GIANT!

Once when Israel battled the Philistines, an enormous man came forward and daily issued a challenge: "Choose a man and have him come down to me. If he is able to fight and kill me, we will become your subjects; but if I overcome him and kill him, you will become our subjects" (1 Samuel 17:8–9). Israel was paralyzed.

Some recurring life issues are not merely pesky, but debilitating. Daily they sap energy and consume time and thought, forming a constant barrier between the present and what God would have a person become. I call these issues the Giants. They have names like

Grief
Chronic Illness or Disability
Addiction
Recent Divorce
Mental Illness
Unemployment
Depression

Every day those giants come out into some lives and roar, "Come fight me. I dare you! Watch me defeat you today!"

If you are fighting a giant Philistine in your life, this book is not and does not claim to be a manual on How to Kill Giants. Books are available that deal with your particular giant, and both support groups and good counselors are available. What I want to say here is this: You will never be able to reduce stress in the rest of your life until you take steps to defeat the power of that giant over your life. That does not mean that you will remove the giant. You may still be chronically ill, have an addictive personality or partner, or grieve. But you can find a way to move beyond focusing on that, so you can focus on God and God's plan for you.

The story of David and Goliath teaches principles that can help you fight your giant.

David's Principle #1: Know You Fight on the Winning Side

David wasn't a better soldier than his brothers, he just believed something they didn't. He fought on God's side, and God can enable us to defeat giants.

When the doctor told Gina she might have cancer, she faced her giant Philistine: fear. She'd wrestled with fear all her life, and knew its potential to incapacitate her as a wife, mother, and nurse. While she waited for her test results, she decided to study and claim the promises of God in Scripture. "For the first time," she says, "I understood what that old hymn meant when it talked about standing on the promises of God. Those promises overcame my fear."

Nancy's giant was her husband's fatal illness. "This was a brilliant man, a gentle man, a man with a terrific sense of humor. We had been married thirty years and expected to grow old together. Then he started having trouble walking, writing, picking up things off the floor. Baffled, he went to the doctor. He had a degenerative brain disease they could do nothing about. I thought as I heard that diagnosis, 'Life is never going to be the same again.' Nobody gets a rehearsal for this. You don't get to practice. I was furious with God—banged my fist on many tables. But God didn't get bowled over by my fury. Instead, God told me, 'I won't leave you. I'm as sad about this as you are. I grieve with you.' The shared grief of God helps me with my own."

God can help us overcome our giants. David trusted that. Gina and Nancy learned to trust it. Do you?

David's Principle #2: Find a Few Good Stones

Good weapons are crucial in battle. David carefully chose five smooth stones. It only took one of them to kill Goliath, but he had several in his pouch, just in case. Women who have defeated particular giants point to resources they have found to be effective weapons.

Prayer

We know that prayer is important in all parts of our lives, but sometimes we hurt too much to frame coherent prayers. Bonnie, who has lived in a wheelchair all her life, says, "I get so tired of hassles that my life entails. But Romans 8:26 means a lot to me when I get frustrated. I know what Paul meant about groans and 'struggles too deep for words.' Some days I groan a lot. It comforts me to know that the Holy Spirit is groaning with me and turning my groans into prayers."

Another useful passage to remember is Exodus 17:8–13, which tells of a battle in which Moses was told by God to hold up his hands in order to insure an Israelite victory. Whenever Moses grew too tired to hold up his hands, two other men held them up for him. Nita writes in an e-mail, "My husband's radiation is so draining for both of us, we can scarcely even pray right now. Please pray for us." When your own giant exhausts you, call on friends to hold up your arms.

When I am too weary to pray coherently, I use prayers I found in Elizabeth Goudge's novel *A Scent of Water.* Goudge tells of a woman who has suffered mental illness all her life. One day she encounters a strange old man who is a fellow sufferer. He gives her three one-sentence prayers to repeat when she is depressed. They are easy to remember and cover all the bases.

Lord, have mercy.
Thee I adore.
Into thy hands.

Individuals Who Have Fought Similar Giants

No matter what giant you are facing, others have faced it before. Ann says, "While I appreciate the sympathy of all my friends, there are times when I need to talk with somebody who has been there—somebody who understands because they've had a child with a chronic illness. They've spent hours in emergency rooms, stood by a child's bed, wondering if they'd make it through the night. They know what I am going through."

If you can't find anyone who has fought your giant, some have shared their stories in print. A visit to a local library or bookstore can arm you with stories that can give you courage to fight.

Support Groups

At a training event for hunger-action enablers—active, committed people—participants invariably strolled in late. One pastor murmured to me, "We must have a lot of adult children of alcoholics in the group." Surprised, I asked what he meant. He held up a small token. "I just finished my first year in an Adult Children of Alcoholics (ACOA) group. Chronic tardiness is something we all struggle with." When I shared his insight with the group, I was amazed how many admitted they grew up with alcoholic parents. Five people wanted to know more about ACOA. They had found a new stone for their own slingshots.

One woman wrote later, "The training event was great, but the best thing I got that weekend was the courage to join an ACOA group and begin to deal with my past."

ACOA is only one of many groups that can help battle giants.

Other women have told me, "I didn't understand how I was involved in my husband's drinking problem until I attended Al-Anon."

"I couldn't have made it through my battle with cancer without my cancer support group."

"I didn't even believe I had a problem until a friend took me to a meeting of Women Who Love Too Much. Hearing other people tell their stories was like reading a script of my life."

"When our baby died, Compassionate Friends got us through."

For almost every giant in the land, we can find a support group to help arm us and to stand with us in the battle. If you aren't sure where to find help, search under "Support Groups" online or in your local yellow pages, ask a pastor, or call a chaplain at a local hospital.

Professional Help

No other stone is a substitute for competent, compassionate professional help when we need it. Professional help for our minds can be as necessary as professional medical help for our bodies.

"We came to a place in our parenting where we knew we didn't have all the answers," says Gail, mother of four. "We sought a counselor and took one child for both counseling and prayer. That turned our family situation around."

David's Principle #3: Choose a Weapon You Trust

David was offered King Saul's own armor, but it was big and unwieldy, and Goliath had a longer arm. Saul's sword wouldn't be of any use. Instead, David relied on the slingshot he'd already used to kill bears and lions.

As we battle giants in our lives, it is crucial for us to find counselors, support groups, physicians, psychiatrists, and authors we can trust, not those who automatically label women "hysterical" or "foolish," those who automatically prescribe drugs rather than treating the cause of illness or depression, or those who do not know the power of God to heal. Like David, we need to battle giants with confidence in our weapons.

One woman spoke of a summer when her teenager was hospitalized in a juvenile psychiatric unit. "We were assigned a psychiatrist who was openly hostile to our faith and who said in no uncertain terms that our child was sick because of my mothering style, that the child would probably never fully recover, and that religion was at the root of many of our problems. He was so sure of himself that we began to doubt ourselves as parents and Christians. We also had to take out a second mortgage on our home so we could go weekly for him to criticize us. For many weeks I prayed in desperate pain. One day I received a call from a woman psychiatrist who was also trained as a Stephen minister, to befriend others in crisis. For weeks she met with me as a friend, cared for me, listened to me, and empathized. Through her support we got the strength to believe again in ourselves and our child, and the wisdom to remove ourselves from the care of that first psychiatrist and find another. Almost immediately, our child began to get better."

The world is full of people who want to offer Saul's armor—weapons that don't fit our particular situation as we battle our giants. However, like David, we need to go into battle with weapons we can trust.

TODAY'S THE DAY

Perhaps as you've read this chapter, you have named your own Philistine and begun to realize it is a gift of God to help you develop strength in your spirit as you battle it in your life. It is given to increase stress in the same way that a personal trainer increases stress to build muscle. Welcome it, battle it, and grow strong.

Maybe you have admitted you are battling a giant, which is what is causing enormous stress in your life, but have told yourself as you read the chapter that you will deal with the giant later. Right now you plan to read on, hoping you'll find help in dealing with all your other stress. PUT DOWN THIS BOOK!

Until you confront and take steps to begin overcoming your particular giant, you cannot get the rest of your life under control. Ask God to help you battle this giant and to show you the first steps to take. Then commit yourself to battle, starting now.

If I know I have a giant in my life causing enormous stress, what is its name? How does it currently limit my life? Whom could I call and ask to hold me accountable as I battle the giant? When will I call that person to set a date to meet and talk about this? What other steps will I take—and when—to start fighting this giant?

- *Call somebody who has battled a similar giant to talk with them. When?*
- *Find a support group and plan to attend its next meeting. When?*

- *Buy a book about a similar giant. When?*
- *Seek a competent counselor and make an appointment. How will I do that? Whom will I ask? When?*

part two

Your Shalom Dream: Perceive It, Plan It

> *Forget the former things; do not dwell on*
>   *the past.*
> *See, I am doing a new thing!*
> *Now it springs up; do you not perceive it?*
> *I am making a way in the desert and*
>   *streams in the wasteland.*
>
> —Isaiah 43:18–19

Picture a Perfect You

Whatever is true, whatever is noble, whatever is right, whatever is pure, whatever is lovely, whatever is admirable—if anything is excellent or praiseworthy—think about such things.

—Philippians 4:8

TRY THIS EXERCISE

Set a timer for one minute. Close your eyes and imagine you are sitting across the table from yourself, but the self across the table is who you would be if you were exactly what God intended you to be on this day and in this place. Look closely at that woman. Ask yourself: "How does she look? What do I see in her eyes? What kind of expression is she wearing? What tone of voice would she use? What is she busy doing in her life, and what is she not busy doing? How is she different from me right now?"

As I have done this exercise with various groups of women, often the first responses when I ask, "What did you see?" are "She is several pounds lighter" or "She had fewer wrinkles." Some women admit they see other differences:

> "Her hair is better cut; her clothes are more stylish; she is proud of herself."

"She is calm. She has the most peaceful expression in her eyes."

"She accepts where she is and makes life happen for her here."

"She smiles a lot more than I do, and doesn't let little things worry her."

One woman even exclaimed, "She wouldn't be a cub scout den mother"—and went home and resigned.

 Do differences between that woman and me reflect yearnings for what I would like to be? What changes do I want to make to bring myself in closer correspondence with what I saw across the table?

If you do this exercise with some frequency, you may be surprised to find yourself becoming more like that woman. Whenever you have a minute of waiting time, close your eyes and picture a perfect you. Our world today lacks heroes and heroines after whom we can model ourselves, but an image of who God created us to be can form one such model for our lives.

A WISE WOMAN KNOWS
If you know what you want to be and do you'll also know what you don't have to be or do.

chapter seven

God's Women Dream BIG

I used to think that Psalm 37:4, "Delight yourself in the Lord and he will give you the desires of your heart," meant that if I delighted myself in God, God would grant my desires. It took me years to realize that God not only *grants* but actually *plants* desires in our hearts. He gives us the desire itself, because he may have a bigger purpose for our desires than we do.

We aren't talking here about trivial things we might like to do—take up skydiving, vacation in Hawaii, win the lottery. Those are wishes, but they are not in the same league with desire.

Desire is that heavy weight we carry deep within us that we may not even be able to name. It is the shadow that lurks in our heart and calls to us in the night, or stings our eyes with tears at unexpected moments. Desire has other names: hope, dreams, yearnings. Often, even if we can name our desire, we may be afraid to hope for it. And we generally don't imagine that our desire was given to us by God or that God has a use for it.

Earlier I spoke about how I yearned to write mystery novels, yet put that dream aside because I was shamed by others into thinking it was not a "holy" desire. When God arranged for me to get back to Chicago so I could write my first mystery, I was grateful to him for making it possible for my dream to come true.

It never occurred to me that *God* could have a use for my writing mysteries.

With one manuscript complete and another begun, I drove from Atlanta, where we were then living, to a national conference of mystery authors and fans in Baltimore. Usually I love to drive long distances alone. It is a great time to pray, relax, and sing aloud without other people laughing. During that trip, though, I was bombarded with the word *serve*. Every radio station from country western to schmaltzy Oldie Goldie was singing about serving somebody. A newscaster reported on high school students who had done a great service project. One of the radio ads that played over and over asked, "How can we serve you?" I saw the word on two billboards.

"I'm not going up there to serve," I reminded myself. "I'm going to look for an agent or an editor for my mystery."

On a deserted stretch of interstate, I passed a stopped car. A young couple stood beside it, and when I saw a baby in the woman's arms as I whizzed past, I sent up a prayer that God would send somebody to stop for them. By the next exit I was so bothered by their plight, I knew I had to turn around and at least offer the woman and baby a ride to the next gas station. When I pulled up beside them, nervous that I was about to get mugged, she told me, "I saw you pass and prayed you'd come back."

Good. I'd done my service project and could get on with my agenda. Yet the word *serve* continued to pound me. Finally I heaved a sigh and said out loud, "Okay, I'll go serve. Maybe I'm not supposed to publish books. Maybe I was just supposed to go to this conference to serve people."

The conference opening party was held in the second floor ballroom of a large hotel. As I got off the elevator, I met a crowd of women coming toward the elevator and heard one say, "I don't want to have to run all the way back up to my room for my coat."

I'm not normally crazy, but I'd been hearing "serve" for two days, so immediately I offered, "Why don't you take mine? I'll be here when you get back." The woman who borrowed my coat turned out to be an author I admire, Nancy Pickard. She has since become a friend.

Inside the ballroom, over a thousand people were milling around, but to me it looked like one big church supper—folks talking in the middle to people they knew, people standing around the edges because they didn't know anybody. Having grown up a preacher's kid, worked for my denomination, and been a preacher's wife, church suppers are situations I feel real comfortable in. I began to move around the edges talking to people and getting to know them. Eventually I met one who apologized, "I'm neither a mystery writer nor reader. I came with my sister who's just published her first book and was scared to come alone." After we talked a while, we made plans to meet for breakfast.

As she, her sister, and I headed down the escalator the next morning talking about breakfast, we heard a voice behind us. "Breakfast? Now that sounds like a good idea. Can we join you?" We were joined by two women who are among my heroes in the writing field. As I sat at the breakfast table, I marveled at how I had gotten to that place.

I was determined not to bring up my own writing, but to "serve" by talking about theirs. Eventually, however, one of them asked, "Do you write mysteries?" The next thing I knew, she had introduced me to her agent, who agreed to look at my book. Within fourteen months my first mystery came out. I was elated at how God had granted the desire of my heart.

Since then, however, as I have gotten to know and love people in the mystery field, I have come to believe that God *planted* that desire in my heart, because the mystery community is one corner of the world into which God has sent me to love and serve. I have made dear friends there and found things I am skilled to do.

"Go into *all* the world," Jesus commanded. How often do we limit that to distant mission fields or local religious places? God wants servants in all parts of the world. God plants desires in our hearts to get us there.

Several years ago I met regularly with a young woman who was the Christian educator in a nearby church. In those years she confided that while she enjoyed what she was doing, particularly working with youth, what she really yearned for was to ride dressage in horseback competitions. She had owned a horse until she left for college and still missed it. This past Christmas we got a letter describing property she and her husband just bought in Virginia horse country, with enough land to build two stalls where she can board and train horses. She wrote, "I am also discipling two teenage girls who own the horses." God needs people in horse country, Virginia. God also needs people in public schools, government offices, and a lot of other places we might not think of until we find ourselves yearning to go there.

The primary thing to remember is that for every person who signs on to live as God's person in God's kingdom here on earth, there is a kingdom job to do and a kingdom place to do it. God knows what that job is and where it needs to be done—and stands ready to assign it.

BIBLICAL WOMEN WHO DARED TO DREAM

Scripture is full of stories of women whose desires God used to achieve wider purposes.

Naomi

The Book of Ruth tells us that Naomi moved from Israel to Moab with her husband and two sons to avoid drought and famine. Her urgent desire was that her family would survive. In Moab her sons took wives and Naomi anticipated grandchildren, until her desire experienced a dreadful setback: both married sons died childless. Naomi returned home with one daughter-in-law, Ruth, and still desired that her family would continue. It was Naomi's plan born of her desire for a family that led Ruth to meet a wealthy relative, Boaz, enchant him in a moonlit field, and eventually marry and produce a child. Thus, Naomi achieved her desire.

Naomi achieved God's purpose, as well. Ruth and Boaz's son, Obed, had a son Jesse, who had seven sons, the youngest of whom was David. Naomi's desire to continue her family led directly to Israel's greatest king and eventually to Jesus. Naomi's desire to save her family from death by famine, even if it meant living in a foreign land, gave David and Jesus a non-Jewish, foreign ancestress, making Jesus kin to the rest of the world.

The Daughters of Zelophehad

Their story is told in Numbers 27:1–11. Because Zelophehad died without sons, his brothers were legally entitled to his estate. His five daughters, desiring security and a place in society, approached Moses and declared that wasn't fair—they ought to inherit. With some humor, Scripture tells us that "Moses brought their case before the Lord." At that time, most cases of this nature were taken to the elders. I picture Moses running his eye over the elders and thinking, "There's no way they can handle this. I'd better take it straight to the Top."

The Lord informed Moses, "What Zelophehad's daughters are saying is right. You must certainly give them property as an inheritance among their father's relatives and turn their father's inheritance over to them." God also says more: " ... this is to be a legal requirement for the Israelites, as the Lord commanded Moses." The daughters of Zelophehad desired security. God desired justice. God used the desire of their hearts to achieve a larger purpose.

Hannah

First Samuel 1 tells how Hannah yearned for a baby and cried out to God. She seems to have understood that her own desires were somehow connected to God's, for she promised that if she bore a child, she would give him back to God's service. Can you imagine giving away your child to be raised by others, far from home? Yet that is an image of what each of us needs to do with our desires if God is to prosper them. First we desire them and beg God to fulfill them, then we hand them back to God to be used for God's own purposes. Hannah's son Samuel grew up in the temple and became the first great prophet of Israel, the one who spoke truth to priests and anointed both Saul and David to be king.

Our dreams and yearnings may be far bigger than we imagine. They may not be merely ours. They may be planted in us by God, who has a purpose for them.

WHEN IS MY DREAM GOD'S DREAM?

Since God made us, it is logical to presume that God's design for the tapestry of each life takes into account exactly who each of us is. One criteria for identifying our deepest dreams was suggested by Joseph Campbell, who devoted his life to the study of myth as a key to human yearnings. Campbell suggested, "Follow your bliss." By that he meant that each of us has certain things that energize us, bring us joy, and make us forget ourselves when we do them. Have you ever gotten so busy doing something that you literally forgot yourself and lost track of time? That is certainly one hint that we are doing what we were created to be doing.

Another hint is found in our strengths and weaknesses—those things we can and cannot do well. And another hint is our wistful longings—those things we either remember fondly or wish we could try, just once. Think about these things:

> *What gives me joy? What energizes me when I do it? What am I good at that I also enjoy doing? What are my strengths as a person? What would I like to do again or do for the first time? What do I wish I could learn to do?*

WHAT PREVENTS US FROM DREAMING BIG?

The saddest thing in the world to me is a person who says, "I don't have any dreams." What I usually find if I dig a bit is that the person has buried those dreams because she or he has no hope they will ever be fulfilled.

Nancy admitted to a young mothers' Bible study group, "I don't have any dreams left. I've got everything I ever dreamed of having: a husband who loves me and three great kids."

Her wise friend Julie asked, "What did you want to be when you were a little girl?"

"A dancer." She answered readily, but then tears filled her eyes. She swiped them away, embarrassed. "I danced all the way through school. In fact, I took my last ballet class the night before I got married. But I'm too old to dance now. My body isn't limber enough, and dancing takes more time than I have to give. I don't have that dream any more."

John Eldredge's book *The Journey of Desire* discusses how frequently in our society we bury our yearnings either by convincing ourselves we are content with what we already have or by trying to satisfy ourselves with fluff: big powerful all-terrain vehicles we never take off the road, romantic vacations that turn out not to be so romantic after all, houses so big we have to leave them vacant most of the day so we can earn enough to pay for them. Meanwhile, deep inside us is a desire for something more, something that really matters to us.

Eldredge argues that we will never find what we desire on this earth and should only anticipate getting it in heaven. While there is truth in that, both Scripture and history demonstrate that God also has plans for us here on earth. As we say yes to our dreams and desires, we find God uses them to enrich the world in amazing ways.

Nancy's story has a happy ending. A few weeks after she claimed she had given up her dream, she came into church all aglow. "There's a liturgical dance class being held next week-end at a church down the road. I've asked my husband to keep the kids so I can go."

She learned liturgical dance and danced for her congregation. She choreographed and taught dances to all the girls, four to eighteen, then she dressed them in long white dresses with garlands on their heads, and they helped lead worship. The last I heard she was teaching a workshop on liturgical dance.

Perhaps God could have used Nancy onstage as a ballerina with a professional troupe. My friend Sheryl Wood sings opera and finds many times and places where she can serve God while she pursues her dream. But God can also shape our dreams to fit our current time and place and use us as we are.

While working on this book, I received two letters from women who participated in a retreat in Canada almost three years before. During that weekend we focused on naming the desires of our hearts, claiming that God had planted them within us, and turning them over to God for God's own purposes. I'll let them tell their own stories.

Marlene: If you remember, when we had the workshop I had my B.A. in art history and three children who were all still at home. I came home knowing that I had to seek God's face more diligently than I ever had. My private devotional time was in great need of discipline. It did not take first place in my day, and I knew that, as a result, I was missing out on so much of what God had in mind for me. Since then, I've come a long way, although there remains much for me to do to reach my goal of a disciplined study and prayer life.

God also impressed upon me the need to develop a personal mission statement, so I chose to give God a day—or however long it took for him to get through to me. The night before, I felt like a little child who was going to Disneyland the next morning. During the night, I woke up several times to the word, "Teach." The following morning I said, "Lord, I don't do *that!* Who and what am I supposed to teach, and where? You have to confirm for me that this is of you."

As I settled myself in my "study" chair and opened my devotional to that day's reference, Numbers 12:6–8 jumped out at me, "I speak to [you] in dreams ... clearly and not in riddles." Could it be any more clear? As I sat in awe and wonder, God and I spent the morning composing my mission statement. It was an absolutely sacred experience. Our time together came to a close with Deuteronomy 30:11–16, which begins, "Now what I am commanding you today is not too difficult for you or beyond your reach." Again, what a confirmation.

But after that, fear took hold of me—fear of failure, and of rejection. After all, I was forty-seven years old. It took me almost exactly one year to finally take action on what I knew I had to do. However, I knew the desire to teach was God-directed, so how could I not proceed?

In order to teach I needed further education. I really didn't want another degree in art history and had a great deal of interest in archaeology, which overlaps art history significantly. I called the archaeology office at the University of Calgary and eventually spoke with two professors whose interests coincide with mine: the study of Mayan culture. I met with them both and really connected with one. Before I left her office, she asked if I could go to Belize with her on a field session for four weeks in May and June. I immediately responded, "I'm sorry, but I have a church women's retreat that I help organize, and I really must be there." Still, for weeks I wrestled with the idea. God finally made me realize that the expectation that I'd run that retreat was my own. Not even I am indispensable. God had put an opportunity in my lap; I had to seize it. To make it easier, God arranged for a woman in the church to come forward and say to me, totally out of nowhere, "Marlene, if you need someone to step in and help with the retreat, I'm there." How much clearer could that be?

Two months ago I submitted my grad school application to the University of Calgary Department of Archaeology and am preparing for my field trip. While I continue to harbor—and hide—fears of rejection and failure, I also know that God has directed me to this point and has plans beyond what I could ever imagine. I hold onto that promise, recognizing that God has an exciting journey just around the corner, and that I will be in the protection of his hands all the way.

Joyce: At the time of our retreat I was at a crossroads, struggling with being disciplined in carving out time for my art, painting, and photography. Even though they were something I loved to do and even felt compelled to do, I let other responsibilities crowd them out. God spoke to me that weekend and awoke a new sense of urgency not to let the creative part of me die a slow death. God reminded me that I have a responsibility to use the gift I have been given. I came away with a renewed excitement, determined to spend some time each day in my studio and to guard that time as important. It was amazing how creativity seemed to flow.

I began painting in oil again after years of doing mainly watercolors. I completed one large and two smaller paintings for an annual art show held in September as a fund-raiser for a local street ministry, and all three of my pieces sold. One of the smaller ones was selected as the best oil painting in the show.

From the proceeds of the sale of the large painting I was able to buy a new camera and have begun selling photo greeting cards, as well.

I am coming to see how God uses our gifts to bring glory to himself and joy to others. My husband, children, and extended family are so supportive and proud. It has also been great for my kids to see this side of me blossom. It encourages them to seek God's best in their own giftedness.

Joyce sent me a generous stack of her greeting cards, and they capture the glory of God in a single flower, a child playing on a beach, and other scenes from nature. Even more beautiful is the knowledge that she is nurturing the desire God planted in her heart and using it for God's own purposes.

WHAT ARE *YOUR* DREAMS?

The rest of this chapter consists of questions women prayerfully asked themselves at that retreat. Like Marlene and Joyce, spend a little time with God exploring your own dreams and the desires of your heart. You may be surprised to discover they are the dreams and desires of God's own heart.

My dream is: (Something that keeps niggling at you, something you have always wished you could do or have recently begun to wish you could do, something that when you think about it, your heart springs up. If you have no dream, spend time today and in coming days listening to the silence. See if God reminds you of a dream you have smothered or buried, or quickens a dream within you.)

What prevents me from dreaming big?

? *Is it*
- *a lack of time, or am I busy about other things? (See Luke 10:38–42)*
- *a lack of money? Do I (we) different priorities for money? (See Matthew 6:21)*
- *other people's needs? Who takes up most of my time? (See Luke 10:27)*
- *fear that I can't succeed? Why do I think I will fail? (See Philippians 4:13)*
- *fear that I might succeed? Why does that scare me?*
- *other people saying I cannot or should not do what I desire to do?*
- *a chronic problem such as sickness, addiction, lack of forgiveness, my past history?*
- *fear to take a risk?*
- *Other:*

? *What scares or worries me about stepping out toward my dream?*

? *If I decide to step out and claim the desire of my heart, what do I see as the greatest obstacles I may have to overcome?*

? *What will I need to give up or change in my current lifestyle to claim the desire of my heart?*

Naming our dream is the first step in achieving it. After that, it's time to get down to the nitty-gritty of getting from here to there.

chapter eight

A Tapestry to Suit Your Style

*Y*our dreams may sound like somebody else's dreams. However, they are threads the Divine Weaver weaves into the tapestry of your life, and your tapestry is not like anybody else's. As Marlene discovered, dreams and the Divine Weaver demand time and commitment from us. As we work together with God, the tapestry begins to assume a pattern that is uniquely our own.

As you set out to achieve your dreams, set aside some time to pray, listen, and write down thoughts that come to you. In addition,

- claim that God made you the way you are, with your own set of preferences, abilities, and limitations, and that what God makes is *good;*
- take a good look at those preferences, abilities, and limitations, so the goals you set are appropriate for who you really are (It is unlikely, for example, that God will call you to run off to join a circus and leave four children behind, but God might take that childhood dream and turn it into a clown ministry for children in the hospital.); and
- consider this current season in your life.

This chapter will help you look at who you are and current seasons of your own life. The following chapter involves concrete planning.

TAKE A HARD LOOK AT YOURSELF

A friend, hearing I was writing this book, sent me a time management book for women that promised if I would put everything—my goals, to-do lists, calendar, Bible study notes, and journal—in one notebook, I could organize my life. I have a friend who is constantly whipping out her palm pilot to enter in another phone number or calendar reminder.

If I did that, I would lose the notebook or palm pilot. That's the kind of person I am.

How organized we are is one way various people are different. Some people feel a need to be very organized. Others spend years getting organized, only to discover they have organized their lives too much. Betty said, "I used to make lists for everything. One day God said to me, 'Betty, lay down your lists.'"

"Did that help?" I asked. "Was that a good thing to do?"

"For me, it was. I was being run by my lists. I had to abandon lists for a time in order to get more prayerfully attuned to God in the course of my day. Instead of having a predetermined day and running on automatic, I began to talk to the Lord step by step. When I started making lists again, I made them prayerfully, and I could use the lists rather than having them use me."

Margaret was married to a man who constantly told her, "You need to get organized. You are dreadfully disorganized." The whole time she was digging clams with her children or learning to upholster furniture, Margaret had that nagging voice at the back of her head, filling her days with stress and unhappiness. Finally she realized she did not need to be more organized, that was who he was, not who she was. Learning who we are and claiming that can help us reduce our own stress, and help us stand up to others who want to shape us in their own image.

As I interviewed women for the original edition of this book, I was struck by how different they were in most things, yet how alike they were in one: each was accomplishing what she felt God called her to be and do.

A WISE WOMAN KNOWS

I may not like what you like or do what you do, because I am not you. God made us different, and that is GOOD.

Elise, an attorney who helped elderly people with estate planning, was a partner in a law firm with offices in three cities. She met with me while she got her nails done— the only "free" hour she planned to have all week. She kept her home highly organized and told me, "What is not essential for me to do, I hire someone else to do. I spend the first hour of every day looking at my calendar, planning with the housekeeper what has to be done, and calling my mother, who does all my shopping. I couldn't live without my calendar. It contains every single thing I need to know and all my phone numbers. I am constantly looking for ways to use time better."

Maxine worked as a medical technologist, served on the county school board, took mission trips to help provide health care, and helped start a local bank. When she and I spent a lazy Sunday afternoon in her living room, she said, "I have an ordered life, but not a particularly disciplined one. I don't plan what I'll be doing in a year or two. One job just seems to follow the next. Because I like mornings, I've arranged to start work at four-thirty. I get up at three, jog, work eight hours, then take an afternoon nap. That leaves a good amount of time for meetings and projects. I concentrate my energy on four areas: education, society, health, and missions. I don't take on responsibilities in other areas."

When I asked about how organized she'd been with their three boys, she grinned. "Sometimes when they were little, we'd get real organized at home, but that usually went out the window. My husband informs me there are people who dust on a regular basis, but I've never been one of them. I'm not much on housework unless there's something special going on."

Of course, "something special" at Maxine's can be a sit-down dinner for forty, a wedding reception in their gorgeous yard, a school-board brunch, or a birthday party for a ninety-seven-year-old friend. Perhaps one reason Maxine doesn't have to clean regularly is that she entertains so often. That works for her.

Gail, a stay-at-home mom, was also an extremely active volunteer in church and community organizations. "I was lucky that my husband's work had regular hours, freeing me to go to evening meetings even when our four children were small. I'd get home late and say, 'Who did the dishes?' He'd answer, 'The parakeet.' Housework always came second with me. My schedule was so irregular, I never had regular days to clean or do laundry. Chores got done when we needed them. The whole family felt that the things I was doing were more important than mopping, and I never believed in spending more time cooking a meal than it took to eat it.

"What I've enjoyed most was starting new programs. I'd get inspired by a need, start a project, then turn it over to other people to run." Among ministries she helped start are a shelter for pre-delinquent teens, a CROP walk for hunger, a Food Bank annual fund-raising banquet, a program to sponsor refugees, and a Bible study program for migrant children.

Bonnie, who lives in a wheelchair, worked for years as part of a Christian education team ministry. Working out of her home to create educational materials, she accomplished more than most people with two functioning legs. She said, "I used to resist a disciplined life because it felt so rigid. I'm a people person, so I wanted to get tasks done so I could be with people. I thought a disciplined, ordered life meant I couldn't take time for people. Now I'm learning what my own order is. I'm a night person, so I have my quiet time at night when nobody is around. I also do office work late—often until two in the morning. I seldom get to my desk before ten, and I schedule people into daytime hours. I have discarded some disciplines I had imposed on myself because I see that they were other people's disciplines, not mine. For a while, on somebody else's recommendation, I tried to spend half an hour each morning in meditative prayer. I learned that not only do I not pray well in the morning, I don't even think clearly in the morning. I also learned that meditation is not a natural way for me to pray. Instead, I have a running conversation with God all day, and meditate when I'm working with plants or cutting vegetables."

These women illustrate that each of us is unique, created by God not only with individual talents and dreams, but also with different rhythms and need for order and discipline.

Who are you, really? In answering the questions below, answer what you are, not what you wish you were. Far too many women are dissatisfied with themselves because they've been told all their lives they ought to be different from what they actually are. God made you as you are and said, "That's good!"

1. When am I at my peak of energy and ambition (best time to work on important things)?
   ❏ very early   ❏ morning   ❏ afternoon   ❏ evening
   ❏ late at night

2. When do I feel the most drained (good time for unimportant tasks)?
   ❏ very early   ❏ morning   ❏ afternoon   ❏ evening
   ❏ late at night

3. In my current schedule, where am I most likely to find time to accomplish my goals?
   ❏ very early   ❏ morning   ❏ afternoon   ❏ evening
   ❏ late at night

4. What is the pace at which I prefer to work on tasks?
   ❏ Dasher (quick)   ❏ Dancer (slow)

5. How do I feel about the pressure of looming deadlines?
   ❏ thrive on it   ❏ don't mind it   ❏ hate it

6. How do I generally complete a task or project?
   ❏ early   ❏ on deadline   ❏ a little late

7. Which do I prefer?
   ❏ working alone   ❏ working with a team
   ❏ working under someone

8. Which best describes the way I *prefer* my days?
   ❏ super-organized and planned
   ❏ moderately disciplined   ❏ spontaneous

9. How do I prefer my home and workplace?
   ❏ neat and organized ❏ cluttered but organized
   ❏ creatively cluttered

10. Which of these do I prefer to do?
    ❏ envision new projects ❏ start new projects
    ❏ carry out projects

11. What do I prefer activities to involve?
    ❏ study ❏ action ❏ interaction with other people
    ❏ service

Now look back at the answers you gave in the last chapter to what brings you joy and energizes you, what your strengths are, and what you yearn to do. As you set goals in the next chapter, keep all these answers in mind. The way you achieve your goals will be different from a woman with the exact same goals but a different personality.

The struggles you face on the way will be uniquely your own too, but everyone faces discouragement and fear along the way. Jesus, remember, went for forty days into the wilderness to pray and think about what he was about to do, and at that time faced three severe tests of his commitment. He also found that God was sufficient and supportive every step of the way.

MORE THAN FOUR SEASONS

As I have spoken with women over the years, I have become keenly aware that women's lives are lived in a succession of seasons. Each woman has a different set of seasons, and a particular season can last a few weeks or several years. Each season has its own particular schedule, responsibilities, and possibilities. Each also has its own set of stresses. And each will eventually end. About the time you are drearily concluding that your entire life will consist of making peanut-butter-and-jelly sandwiches or going to a particular job, your last child goes to college or the job ends, and you find yourself on the threshold of a new season.

> There is a time for everything, and a season for every activity under heaven.
>
> —Ecclesiastes 3:1

Seasons are defined by words like "until" or "as long as" or "before," and come in two basic sizes: long and short. A long season can last a year or several years; short ones can last a few days or a few weeks. Here is a far-from-exhaustive list of sample seasons other women have named. Do you recognize any as your own?

Long season examples. *From now until...*	Short season examples. *From now until...*
my last child starts school	my child's ballet or piano recital
one child is able to drive	this sports season ends
my children are all in college	I meet my deadline
I change jobs/my husband changes jobs	my husband with Alzheimer's can no longer relate to me
I move from this town, church, or house	my term in office ends
my parents are no longer alive/no longer live with us	this semester is over/summer vacation is over
I get my degree	I make a particular major decision

(Chart continues on following page)

Long season examples. *From now until...*	Short season examples. *From now until...*
I retire	a particular project is completed
I lose my health	I recover from a recent illness
I can no longer live alone	I get through this time of grief

Note that some of those seasons are determined by other people, and some by the women themselves. If you intend to set goals you can accomplish, remember that your seasons often depend on people who matter to you, and set your goals accordingly.

Note also that some seasons have predictable ends—when children go to school, when we retire. Others have nebulous ends—as long as I have my health, while we live in this town. In the next chapter we will consider how to set goals for both.

Obviously each of us lives in several seasons simultaneously. I have found, therefore, that as women set goals, they are foolish to set them for ten years, five years, or one year. Women don't live like that. We are wiser to set long-range goals for our longest season and short-range goals for short or mini-seasons in between.

To give a personal illustration, I wrote the revised edition of this book in two sometimes conflicting mini-seasons: "until this book is finished" (approximately six weeks long) and "until we move" (approximately eight weeks long). Each shaped my daily schedule and gave me particular responsibilities and opportunities. In addition, as I've said before, we have just begun a long, undefined season of "as long as Bob's mother lives with us." That makes demands on my schedule, gives me new responsibilities, and provides new opportunities. In terms of my long-range season, however, as a woman in her late fifties, I expect that some faculties may diminish significantly enough in coming years to curb what I can do. Because there are things I want to be sure I accomplish and places I want to go before I am physically less able to do and go, I've chosen to set my long-range goals for "Before I turn 65."

 What is currently my longest definable season? How long is it likely to last? What short seasons am I currently in? How long will each of them last?

A WORD OF WARNING

Do as I say, not as I recently did. I regularly tell women, "Whenever you are about to enter a new season, take time to think about it and plan what you want to do and become in that season."

Yet when our younger son went to college, I didn't follow my own advice. I joked that I could do a lot of things in the hours I used to spend waiting for him to come in at night. Subconsciously, after twenty-one years of constant child-rearing, I felt I now had all the time in the world for long-deferred plans and dreams. Impulsively I accepted the office of treasurer in an organization with financial difficulties, accepted a three-year part-time position helping to plan a national denominational emphasis, offered to write our church's newsletter, and decided to get my master's degree. Of course, I also continued to write and promote books, teach a church school class, and chair our congregation's active hunger committee. Within a year my husband decided we ought to move closer to town, so I added a move to the mix. The closest I got to a vacation in three years was when I fell off a chair and sprained an ankle so badly I had to keep it up for a week.

I discovered two things I'll pass along. First, the principles in this book really do work. If I hadn't known them, I could not have gotten through the first semester of 2001, when I had to write my master's thesis, revise a book, plan the promotion of another book, complete two classes, and wind up my work with the denomination. At one point I called my parents and told them, "Plan to come down the first weekend in May, but I don't know yet if you'll be here for my graduation or my funeral."

"That's okay," Dad replied. "In either case, I'll need my good black suit."

The suggestions I give in the last four chapters of this book are what got me through those hectic days.

The second thing I want to say again is what I knew but apparently needed a refresher course in: We let ourselves in for a lot of stress when we accept tasks and responsibilities without first taking them to God and prayerfully mulling over whether that particular "real good thing to do" is also *my* thing to do. There is a time and season for every purpose under heaven, but I personally do not have to do everything under heaven—in this or any other season.

chapter nine

What's Your Plan?

*T*hree small brothers were talking. Philip, five, asked Jesse, seven, "What do you want to be when you grow up?"

"An architect," Jesse replied.

Andrew, three, propped his fists on his hips, indignant. "Philip didn't ask what you want to *do*, Jesse. He asked what you want to *be*."

Andrew offers wisdom to all who want to set goals.

WHY SET GOALS AT ALL?

The first time I set goals was in 1975. My husband— weary of being a "patron of the arts" for a writer who spent most of her time reading other people's books, serving on boards and committees, or having lunch with friends— requested accountability. I sat down and drew up elaborate five-year goals describing an ever-increasing commitment to writing for income. I included serving on hunger committees I felt God wanted me to serve on. I included both faith growth and time to be with friends. "Here," I said. "Here are my goals."

I did not include having two babies.

When our first child was born in 1977, I nearly wore us both out staying on schedule. In the three months before he was born, I completed a commissioned full-length play and a thirteen-week church school curriculum. In his first four months I wrote a book of hunger education games, often typing at 3 A.M. while he dozed beside me in his swing. I dragged him to hunger meetings and workshops all over the country. I was often irritable, exhausted, and so busy being efficient that I missed some of the fun of mothering. When he turned one, I cut back my writing to three mornings a week and dropped most committees. When the second child came along in 1980, I put my goals in a drawer and forgot them.

I found them in 1989 while cleaning out files. To my utter surprise, I discovered I had accomplished every one. Granted, it took me fourteen years, not five, but even when I was unconscious of them, they were buried in my memory and charted my direction. Those goals were not just about something I wanted to do, but about something I wanted to be: a practicing professional writer. So even while I was working on something else I wanted to be—a loving mother—those first goals shaped decisions I made about how to spend time and energy when the children didn't need me. In fact, I think I was a better mother because I wasn't absorbed only in the children.

SILENCING CRITICAL VOICES

This chapter is not so much about our destination as about our journey, the *process* of getting to the place where we establish goals for our lifetime, for long and short seasons, and for each particular month. Before we begin, though, we must silence three whispering voices who will try to defeat us.

Voice One: "You don't have time to set goals and plan."

The truth is, we are too busy *not* to plan. If we don't name our goals—what we want to do— then we won't know what we *don't* want to do. No matter how many tips we master for freeing time in our busy days, we won't relieve much stress, because we'll tend to fill that free time with more things we don't want to do. Remember, stress does not come from being busy.

A WISE WOMAN KNOWS

If you don't know where you want to go you will never know whether you get there.

Stress comes from being busy about things we don't want to do or from not being busy about things we do want to do.

Voice Two: "Setting goals and planning how to achieve them are too complicated."

Nonsense. Each one of us sets goals and plans how to accomplish them every day of our lives. Cooking a meal involves setting a goal—putting a meal on the table—and planning the necessary steps to achieve that goal. Dressing for the day involves setting a goal—getting dressed—and planning steps to achieve that. We aren't talking about rocket science in this chapter, we are talking about expanding a process every one of us already knows how to do.

Voice Three: "People who trust God shouldn't set goals and make plans. We are supposed to wait on the Lord for guidance."

This voice is the most insidious, because it sounds so holy. It also contains a great truth: We do indeed need to listen to God as we make our long-range goals and plan our days. But does that mean we don't set goals and make plans? Of course not.

We've already discussed how Naomi, eager to become a grandmother and perpetuate her family's line, laid careful plans to bring her beautiful widowed daughter-in-law to the attention of a wealthy relative.

Nehemiah also planned. Scripture tells us there were two months between the time when he first heard that the walls of Jerusalem needed restoration and the day he went to the king's table (where he served as "cup bearer," or taster, to make sure the king wasn't being poisoned) looking sad enough that the king asked, "What's wrong?" We can deduce that Nehemiah had been planning, because immediately he whipped out detailed lists of everything he was going to need to restore the walls.

Esther planned. Challenged to stop the imminent destruction of Jews in her husband's kingdom, she spent three days in prayer, fasting, and planning, then executed a marvelous plan to bring down the wicked Haman and save her people.

Jesus thought people needed to plan. In Luke 14:28–33, he compares deciding to follow him with the process of building a tower or making war, situations that require a good deal of planning. His parables praise wise stewards who set goals of increasing the master's money and making plans to carry through; wise virgins with a goal of waiting for the bridegroom, who plan how to keep their lamps lit until he arrives; even a crafty steward who plans for his future after he gets fired. When the Spirit told Jesus the time was ripe, he *planned* to go to the cross. Luke 9:15 tells us that in spite of his disciples' objections, "As the time approached for him to be taken up to heaven, he *resolutely* set out for Jerusalem." He had also laid careful plans for how to celebrate his last Passover with the disciples and reserved a private room.

Granted, we must hold our plans lightly, knowing that the Spirit may blow a wind through them at any moment and make drastic changes. Acts 16 tells how Paul planned to go to Bithynia, but the Spirit sent him to Macedonia instead. Note, however, that Paul was not sitting around waiting for instructions when the Spirit intervened. Note too that when Paul planned to go to other places, like Corinth and Athens, he went.

The fact is, all of us—including those who claim they do not—actually make long-range plans. We pore over patterns for bridal dresses and plan menus for wedding receptions. We collect brochures for vacation destinations and plan our trips. We spend hours planning women's conferences and retreats. We plan projects at work. The only thing we are content to muddle through without plans is life itself.

GETTING DOWN TO GOAL SETTING

I have found it helpful to set up on my computer four permanent pages in a "Goals" file.* If you aren't using a computer, four sheets of paper work equally well. Label them with the following titles:

- Lifetime Goals
- Long-Season Goals
- Short-Season Goals (or, if you prefer, Annual Goals)
- This Month's Tasks

I also find that because our lives are lived in several arenas simultaneously, it is important to set goals for each important arena. If we focus only on one, we can sabotage the others. Conversely, arenas we ignore have a potential to sabotage our goals in others. Therefore, on each page, list the arenas of your life and set at least one goal for each. My own goals fall under these headings:

*A Sample Goals Worksheet can be found on page 187.

- Personal (spiritual and physical goals)
- Professional
- Family (marriage, parenting, and household goals)
- Church and Community

And before setting your goals, remember three things:

Goals are precious. Handle with prayer. Before setting something as serious as a goal for your life or even for a season, ask God to help with this process and give you wisdom.

Goal-setting is a soul-stretching exercise. Goals are based on our deepest desires, not just our current abilities. We are looking out to our farthest horizon and asking, "What is possible for me? What do I most want to do in this season? What will I most regret not having done?"

Goals are never set in stone. Even lifetime goals may change as we age. One mother told me, "For a while, with two sets of twins under four, my lifetime goal was to get all my children out of diapers and into school. Now that three of them are married, my goals have altered a lot."

I once set as my Family goal: "To raise boys who become Christian men capable of taking care of their own needs and the needs of others." To that end, I taught them all sorts of household skills, took them regularly to church, and read them Bible stories and prayed with them each night.

When a wise friend pointed out that we cannot raise Christians, we can only expose children to our faith and hope they will adopt it as their own, I changed my goal slightly.

Then at a retreat, a leader asked, "If you were to die in six months, what would you most want to make sure you had done?" Immediately I knew: "Enjoy my children." At that second, I didn't care if I taught them another thing. I saw that I had been so focused on teaching I had laid aside the fun of being with them. That changed my goal. It became "To enjoy our two sons and raise them to be God-conscious men who know they are loved, who are equipped to care for their own needs, and who have experienced what it is like to care for others." And because our family tends to be workers, not players, for each month while the boys were growing up I put on my monthly goals, "Plan at least one fun event with the whole family."

Lifetime Goals

As little Andrew knew, lifetime goals are not so much about what we want to do, but about what we want to eventually *be*. One way to think about lifetime goals is to ask, "By the time I die, what do I want to have accomplished and/or become?" Another way to ask it is, "When I die, what will I most regret if I have not done or become?"

I once read that "The greatest tragedy in life is not to be a saint," so I have taken "To become a saint" for my personal goal, adding, "by which I mean to learn to know, love, and trust God and to let God channel his love and power through me to others." Other personal goals women have shared with me include:

> "To be someone who serves others and makes a real difference in their lives."
>
> "To know God deeply, not just as a mediocre Christian, and to find out who I am in him."
>
> "To leave my children with a good relationship with me and with the Lord."

What do I want to be or have accomplished by the time my life is over? Asking for God's help, stretching myself to my farthest horizon, remembering what it is I dream and yearn to do, and knowing that these goals may change in months and years to come, what do I identify right now as lifetime goals for each of the major arenas of my own life?

Long-Season Goals

Goals for each long season spring from lifetime goals and move us a little closer toward them. In seasonal goals, we bite off a smaller piece of each lifetime goal—bites appropriate to this particular season in our life. We may focus on one thing more heavily and almost completely postpone working on another lifetime goal because this is not the season for that.

Betty said, "My ultimate goal is to be God's person, dedicated totally to knowing and serving God. But God has revealed times and seasons for other goals. It was as if a spotlight came and focused on me. At one time parenting was it. We had recently moved to Britain, and four of our six children were still young. My husband needed to return to the States frequently to meet previously made commitments. Things were in such an upheaval that I realized I had to focus on being an absolute anchor for the children. My focus was to provide security for them." I would add that Betty is a noted composer, but at that particular season she was composing music in parking lots while waiting for her children to finish a practice or event.

She continued, "At a later season I was led to establish a music business to provide a good bit of income for the Community of Celebration, the religious community in which we lived. God kept giving me ideas and visions for how that could work, and it was the key to our financial security in those days. God showed me how to make it happen.

"During a period when the community was planning to relocate and we had come back to the United States as forerunners, my husband suffered a heart attack. I had been centered on music, our family, and the community for years, but at that time God indicated I was to be involved in outreach for a season. For three to four years I traveled quite a lot internationally, keeping networks open.

"Still later, God centered me on the maturing life of the community, being available to the community and to our growing ministry within our denomination."

That's as far as Betty had come when we spoke for the first version of this book. Since then she has experienced several additional seasons. She lost her husband, cared for her elderly mother and aunt for a season, remarried for a few years, then lost that husband. She is now winding up his affairs and once again seeking God's direction for this new season in her life.

"How do you know if you are doing what God wants you to do in a given season?" I asked.

She smiled. "God gives a discernible peace in the context of life, a peaceable presence along the way. Ideas are given, doors are opened. God gives forward movement."

God's forward movement in our lives. That's what we are talking about—believing God's promise in Jeremiah 29:11: "I know the design I am weaving for you, a design of *shalom* and not for harm, to give you a future with hope" (my paraphrase).

As you set seasonal goals, obviously you have both long-term and short-term seasons. First set goals for the period between now and the time when your life will change most radically in terms of schedule, responsibilities, and opportunities—a period such as "Between now and the time all my preschoolers leave home" or "As long as I work at this job." Later is the time to refine your goals further, setting a direction for this year, this month, or for shorter seasons, such as "Until summer vacation is over" or "Until I finish this deadline."

Here are samples of some long-season goals other women have set:

- To complete my college degree before my children start college.
- To increase my professional competence before my children are all in school, so I can find a job.
- To find one significant way to help the poor in my community as long as we live in this town.
- To make our home a place of peace and welcome for ourselves and others while all the children are at home.

As I look at my current season (named in the previous chapter) and goals I have tentatively set as my lifetime goals, what do I most want to accomplish in each arena of my life during this particular season?

Goals for Shorter Seasons

Some women—and I am usually one of them—write annual goals as they work through a particular long season. Gloria and her husband take a vacation between Christmas and New Year's and write goals both personally and for their marriage. Other women prefer to set goals not for a year, but for one short season at a time: "Until I finish my term as president of the Garden Club," "During this summer school break," "Until I achieve my next promotion."

As I look at my lifetime goals and long-term seasonal goals derived from them, what do I want to accomplish in this next year or shorter season of my life in each of my life's arenas? What will I most regret not having done? What is the length of time for which I am setting these short-term goals? From now until . . .

Are there any goals I am intentionally postponing for a later season?

Tasks to Accomplish This Month

Now is when the rubber hits the road—when we look at all those wonderful things we want to accomplish and try to fit them into this next month. That means biting off small bits we can do, tasks we can accomplish, plans we think we can accomplish in the next thirty days.

What small, doable tasks will I do to move myself toward each of my goals in this coming month?

This is the first month in which you will need to begin stopping some of what you have been doing in order to make time to achieve your goals, so it is also important to ask:

What will I need to stop doing or decide not to do, in order to accomplish this month's more desirable tasks?

REMEMBER . . .

This chapter describes a *process* for moving toward the person you want to become. None of what you have written here is carved in stone. The Goal Setting Team will not come to your house if you fail to achieve all that you have planned or if you change your mind. Bonnie said, "Once I went through an elaborate process of setting goals. I decided I wanted a second master's degree. I planned exactly what I had to do to get the degree, how I would pay for it, and what I would have to change in my life in order to have time for classes. A week later I realized I didn't want that degree at all. But going through the process helped me clarify what I did want to do instead."

Therefore, focus not just on the final product but also on the process. Post your lifetime goals where you can see them often and refine them in months to come. Develop a habit of writing goals for upcoming seasons and for each month— checking back to see what your lifetime, long- and short-term season's goals are before you set the month's goals.

If you find that in one area of your life you consistently are not meeting your goal, ask whether that goal is one you really want to achieve. Possibly it needs some major rethinking.

Another thing that needs serious consideration is this: Now that you've got your goals, can you afford them?

chapter ten

How Can You Pay for Your Dreams?

Many woman don't think much about managing money and are content to let others do that for them. However, many of our goals, such as travel, further education, starting a business or ministry, recreation, and retirement, are expensive. If God inspired the goal, God will help us finance it, but that is seldom a magical process whereby gold coins are dropped into our lap. An important part of setting goals is looking at our related financial picture.

> Jesus said, "Suppose one of you wants to build a tower. Will he not first sit down and estimate the cost to see if he has enough money to complete it?"
>
> —Luke 14:28

LOOKING INTO THE HOLE OF DEBT

Before we start talking about financing goals, we need to talk about debt, because taking control of our lives *must* involve taking responsibility for our debts. No matter how well we state our goals and plan our days, if our credit card bill each month is more than we can pay, we are going to live under stress. So are our heirs, if we don't pay the debts. I am astonished at how many people think debts die with them.

Trying to save toward goals without paying your debts, therefore, is like trying to swim out of a whirlpool. You may work hard and think you are making progress, but you get sucked down the drain in the end.

There are several ways we can pay off debts:

- put away credit cards to keep from increasing debt and set aside money from each paycheck to pay current debt
- take a second job until debt is paid
- use savings or sell investments, if credit card interest is more than earnings on investments or savings
- refinance a home to pay off other debts and add that sum to the mortgage if mortgage interest is lower than credit card interest
- for really overwhelming debt, talk to a credit counselor or financial planner

Whatever it takes, work to eliminate debt so your money can go where your dreams are.

HOW CAN I FINANCE MY GOALS?

There are a limited number of ways to get money. Stealing is immoral, winning a lottery is unlikely, and inheriting is unpredictable, so we are left with four likely alternatives:

increase income
redirect spending habits
save regularly
invest wisely

Increase Income

Most of us are going to need to earn more if we have goals that need financing. Sadly, women's income is still roughly 75 percent of what men earn in comparable positions, and the lowest-paid workers, both men and women, hold jobs traditionally filled by women, such as child care workers, teachers, secretaries, directors of Christian education, church musicians, and domestics. One question for a woman seeking to meet her goals must be, "Can I make enough doing this job to achieve my goals?" If not, it's time to rethink your job.

Jayne, a single mom who wanted a home for her children, left a small bookstore that paid minimum wage and went to a large chain store that paid more plus benefits and where she was eventually promoted to store manager. Cathy, who wanted to stay home until her children went to school, originally took in other children for very little pay. When she realized she wanted to go to college and become a teacher, she decided to get certified as a child care worker, have her home licensed, and charge market rates for her services.

Each of these women prayerfully set goals that required more money than they could earn in their current employment. Each took steps to earn more. If you find that your goals and your income aren't compatible, consider changing jobs. If you earn nothing and your goals will require funds, consider making a deal with your parents or spouse: they give you a loan now and you pay it back when you are better able. Also consider upgrading your skills or completing a degree to qualify you for a higher salary. Investment in education and training today can result over the years in significantly greater earnings.

Redirect Spending Habits

Redirect spending habits toward meeting goals. A lot of families are working themselves to death trying to have a better life. Women frequently tell me that it takes two wage-earners to support their family, but how many of us are working too hard to buy more things we don't need or use? In the process, we sacrifice our sanity and our families. We may even endanger our health and our lives.

We buy bigger houses than we need, then leave them vacant most of our waking hours because we have to work so hard to pay for them and their furnishings. We buy enormous cars and use them to transport one or two people. We fill our closets with clothes we don't wear, magazines we don't read, exercise equipment we don't use, and sports equipment we seldom have time to play with. In a perfect world we would use our income to achieve our goals and reduce our stress. In the real world, money-related stress is consuming us. We exchange the hours of our lives for things, yet the things don't make us happy.

A look at your checkbook for the past year may uncover places you are currently spending money that could be applied toward your goals. Mary had never noticed how often her family ate out until she printed up a computer report of her annual expenditures by categories. Carol was flabbergasted by how much she spent in one year on Internet impulse purchases. Susan looked at her clothing expenditures and resolved to shop in consignment shops for a year in order to save toward one of her goals. Michelle considered her insurance premiums and how seldom her family was ill and decided to take a higher deductible. Sarah and her husband moved into a smaller home and cut their mortgage and insurance payments in order to finance her dream.

Jesus says that wherever our treasure is, our hearts will be also. The reverse is also true: wherever your heart is, direct your treasure in that direction. A good question to keep in front of you is, "How can the money I earn and/or spend be best directed toward accomplishing my life goals?"

Married couples need to ask that question together concerning joint goals. Wise couples also recognize that partners have individual goals, and allot money for each to spend on those goals. Consider two different scenarios:

Jack wanted a new computer so he could occasionally work from home. Marilyn wanted a car so she could accept a job some distance away. Both agreed to buy what they wanted from family funds. However, she felt he bought more computer than they needed, even though she enjoys using it sometimes for her own work, and he thought her new car—a sporty model—was too pricey, although he always drives it on weekends.

Steve wanted a small sailboat for family recreation. Sarah wanted a trip to renew family ties in San Francisco. Each receives a personal allowance from family funds to use for books, clothes, personal items, *and* to achieve personal goals. Within six months Sarah saved enough in her account for a few days in San Francisco and took Steve along. Steve scrimped on books and clothes for a year, bought a sunfish, and the family now sails each weekend. They each had the pleasure of both achieving a goal and treating their spouse.

A WISE WOMAN KNOWS
What I earn and what I spend ought to enhance my goals, not sabotage them.

If those sound like scenarios for "Can This Marriage Be Saved?" one of them almost was. In the realm of marriage finances, some private money for each partner reduces an enormous amount of stress.

Save Regularly and Invest Wisely

Saving regularly can help move you toward your goals, but investing wisely speeds up the process. Savings accounts earn little interest these days. Mutual funds and stocks can earn more—but only if you are willing to learn a bit about investing. If you are nervous about investing,

- take an investment course at a local community college. The money you invest in one good course will be quickly repaid by wise investment.
- join an investment club and learn how to invest with other women. One group devoted to women is Chicks Laying Nest Eggs. A book with the same title tells how ten women began an investment club years ago, which has become an international organization with many chapters. The website, www.chickslayingnesteggs.com, offers resources for groups just starting up.
- read books by financial wizards. Two good ones I've enjoyed recently are *Rich Dad, Poor Dad* by Robert T. Kiyosaki and *Smart Women Finish Rich* by David Bach. Each makes a clear connection between goals and finances.

GETTING OUR PRIORITIES IN ORDER

Whatever our goals, we need to hold all our money both lightly and thankfully.

Bonnie prays as she writes monthly checks, thanking God for whatever she is paying for and praying for those who receive her check. "An attitude of gratitude lets me enjoy some purchases twice and notice blessings I generally forget, like electricity and water."

Gail points out that tithing "is a discipline that seems to order the rest of our lives."

Shirley made perhaps the closest connection between her goals, God's goals, and her money: "I feel God is telling me to spend time with my grandchildren as they are growing up. I dream of having a fish camp one day where we can go fishing together. That takes money, just as sending four children to college earlier took money. I work in order to earn money to finance my dreams. But I try to remember that it is God's money, just as my time and talents are God's time and talents. All are given to me to be used in God's way."

> **?** *Which of my goals will require money? How much money will each require?*

> **?** *Where will I get the money to accomplish each goal? How long will it take to get it?*

> **?** *If debt hinders my meeting other goals, what steps do I need to take to get out of debt? How soon can I accomplish that?*

part three

Weaving Your Dreams into Reality

> *This day is sacred to our Lord. Do not grieve, for the joy of the Lord is your strength.*
>
> —Nehemiah 8:10

chapter eleven

Getting a Handle on Today

Setting goals is not our biggest problem. Our biggest problem is generally living them out *today*.

An old joke has the devil asking little demons how to best destroy the human race. The prize goes to the imp who suggests, "Let's assure them they can become everything God wants them to be—starting *tomorrow*."

If only today weren't so cluttered with calls we need to make, errands we need to run, old habits we need to break, and commitments we need to honor. How can we possibly live out new plans and goals, set out on the journey to accomplish our dreams, when we're already swamped?

We can't. That's why our first step is to take authority over today.

To do that, we must become intentional about how we spend our time. That doesn't mean we will be busy all the time. We may be intentional about taking out quiet times to pray and put our feet up. We may be intentional about playing more with children. We may be intentional about leaving undone some things we always have done, because we have realized they are not things God has given us to do. We will hopefully be intentional about making sure we work on our goals. We will be intentional about trying to kick habits that defeat us. We will be intentional about which commitments we accept and which current ones we gently release. The key word is *intentional*.

Remember the Latin phrase *Carpe Diem,* "Seize the Day"? Gordon MacDonald coined a related phrase, "unseized time"—time over which we have not taken authority. He argues convincingly that unseized time will most naturally flow in four directions:

- toward things we do least well, which therefore take the most time to do;
- toward the demands of dominant people in our life;
- toward crises and emergencies; and
- toward what gives us the most public acclaim.*

I would add,

- toward the piddlies, those mundane tasks we all have to do, but which easily take over our lives if we let them.

If we are not intentional about how we spend our days, we will be most likely to spend all our time on the urgent, the impressive, the complicated, the most demanding, and the piddlies. What will get neglected are the quiet, important things we have always wanted to do, but somehow never find the time for. In other words, what gets neglected are our own goals and dreams. Why? Because they are least likely to clamor for attention, cause crises or emergencies, or matter to others.

---

*Gordon MacDonald, *Ordering Your Private World* (Nashville: Nelson, 1985), 7.

KICKING THE HABIT

Old habits are hard to break, but if we are honest, we will see that we developed a number of them to compensate for not achieving our goals. Isn't that a paradox? Some of the very things that keep us from achieving our goals are in our lives because we subconsciously believed we would never be able to realize our deepest dreams, so we sought other ways to pamper ourselves. Some women watch too much television. Some talk too much on the phone. Some drink or eat too much. Some get too engrossed in handwork. Some shop compulsively. Some read too much. All of these things can consume valuable time we can use instead to move toward our goals.

> *As I start out on the journey toward accomplishing my goals, what habit(s) do I need to change in order to have time to do what I most value?*

COMMITTING TO FEWER COMMITMENTS

Obviously when we set new goals and plan to head in new directions, we need to adjust former commitments to bring our lives into line with our goals. However, this needs to be done gently. People still depend on us to do what we've said we will. One important step, then, is to look at all our current commitments and prayerfully decide which we want to keep, which we want to reduce our commitment to, which we can drop immediately, and which we will drop as soon as a term runs out or a project is completed.

A WISE WOMAN KNOWS
To make a successful journey you cannot keep running in circles.

What current commitments will I need to eliminate or reduce in the coming year in order to achieve my goals? When will I make that change for each commitment?

DON'T LET THE PIDDLIES GET YOU DOWN

Mundane tasks—things nobody puts on her goal list but most of us must do, like washing dishes and keeping the bathroom hygienic—take up sizeable parts of our day. In fact, if you stop and add up the minutes you spend in a year doing mundane tasks—grocery shopping, cleaning, running the same errands—you may be astonished. Consider this chart:

Minutes per Day	Minutes per Week	Hours per Year
5	35	30
15	105	90
30	140	120
60	280	240

Can you believe that five minutes a day making your bed adds up to thirty hours a year? Five-minute tasks eat up our lives in a hurry unless we take intentional steps to control them. Therefore, one assignment if we truly want to accomplish our goals is to consider how to reduce the amount of time we spend on mundane tasks, freeing time to meet our goals. Some possibilities:

- *Ask other family members to pull their own share of the mundane task load around the house.* This may require some training, but you may be surprised to discover somebody else in your family enjoys tasks you have found onerous.*
- *Restrict mundane tasks to times when you are not at your best.* Try to save your personal peak times for more important things. A corollary of that is *reserve your best energy.* If your most important event of the day is later in the day, don't spend the morning cleaning house so you are too tired for the important activity.
- *Set lower standards for cleanliness.*
- *Hire a maid.* If you are serious about accomplishing your goals and can possibly afford it, hire someone who needs the income to clean the house at least once every two weeks. Both of you will benefit.

 What changes do I need to make so that mundane tasks and errands don't consume too much of my day?

Remember, you are not trying to squeeze minutes out of your day, but to refocus your life to spend more time on what you most value.

WHIPPING YOUR TO-DO LIST INTO SHAPE

Taking authority over our day involves thinking through what we plan to do today. That's not merely drawing up a to-do

---

*My companion book to this one, *Children Who Do Too Little,* describes how to build a family team to care for the family's house.

A WISE WOMAN KNOWS

"Besides the noble art of getting things done, there is the noble art of leaving things undone."
–Lin Yu Tang

list of things other people think are important, errands we need to run, and mundane tasks we need to accomplish, then breathing a sigh of relief when we've checked them all off.

Unless, of course, your primary life goal is to make the *Guinness Book of Records* as The Woman Busiest about the Most Trivial Things.

For the rest of us, taking authority over our days means arranging each day to spend prime time on what we value most.

Our to-do lists need to feature things that are important to us, things we want to make *sure* we accomplish today, even if we have to let a few crises resolve themselves, other people handle some of their own emergencies, and errands get put off for another day. Here are a few skills to help us focus on what is important.

Learn the 3-Ds

Drop items on your to-do list that

- will not matter if they never get done,
- you have committed to but know you cannot do well, and
- you truly do not want to do.

A growing place in my own life is to learn to prayerfully listen to my aversions, and to know God also speaks through them. That meeting we dread going to or the office we hate fulfilling may be God saying, "I have other things for you to do with your time. Somebody else will fill that office and sit on that committee."

Just this past month I experienced a humorous—in retrospect—example of God working through an aversion. Nearly a year ago I agreed to teach a series of mini-workshops on my book *Women Home Alone* one Saturday, not realizing how busy I was going to be during this particular month. As the time drew near, I could not make myself prepare for that event. I'd get out my notes, then remember something else I needed to do. Even the night before the event, I could not make myself really study the notes. "I know all this," I decided and went to bed. But since normally I prepare carefully for events, my aversion to preparing for that one actually surprised me, and I arrived a little nervous the next morning.

If I'd known what was about to happen, I'd have been more nervous. It was every speaker's worst nightmare. When I finally was handed a program, it announced that I would be leading three one-hour workshops not on Women Home Alone, but on Women Who Do Too Much.

That was not what we agreed on. I never teach this topic in an hour because it can't be done effectively. My notes from the invitational call clearly show they asked me to speak on Women Home Alone. Some time between our conversation and the time they printed the program, somebody changed the topic. God knew that—and that I didn't have time to spend preparing for a workshop I didn't have to teach. My aversion was God saying, "Don't waste your time."

I was immensely grateful that at least God nudged them to have me teach something I've been so immersed in for weeks

A WISE WOMAN KNOWS
The 3-Ds of daily management: Drop, Delay, *and* Delegate.

that I could outline a speech in the forty-five seconds I had between the time I saw the program and needed to begin my first workshop.

Delay anything on your to-do list that

- you can put off until another time, or
- will take longer to work on than you have in this particular day.

My personal theory is, don't do anything before you have to; that way, if you die before you need to do it, you won't have wasted precious living time doing something you didn't need to do. Delaying, however, is *not* the same as procrastinating. To delay means to put off something until it needs to be done. To procrastinate means putting it off until past the time when it needs to be done.

The time by which something "needs to be done" differs for different personality types. Some people work best under pressure, others are paralyzed by pressure. You know which is true for you, so set your "delay until . . ." schedules accordingly.

At one workshop several participants told me their pastor was "a terrible procrastinator" because he never finished his sermon until late Saturday night. When I asked him if he procrastinated in preparing sermons, he said, "Maybe so, but the sermon jells best for me then. I like the pressure." He seemed relieved when I suggested he didn't procrastinate, he delayed.

Delegate items on your to-do list that

- someone else could do almost as well as you,*

---

*Obviously they cannot do it quite as well or better, or they'd be doing it. Right?

- someone else has more skill to do,
- someone else has more time to do.

Maxine charmingly refers to delegation as "Inviting others to be involved in the good things I am doing." She gave this example: "A woman in our church was overwhelmed by having to take her husband to daily chemotherapy. I felt so sorry for her, I offered to do it every day for a week, then checked my calendar and found I was busy every single day that particular week. I called five other women in the church, explained what needed to be done, and why I couldn't do it. They could, and did."

I suspect some of the women she called were honored to be asked to share in what she was doing. You might not believe it, but I am frequently told by women who do *not* come to my workshops, "I don't do too much. I don't even do enough. Nobody ever asks me."

One day I invited an elderly member of our congregation to lunch in spite of the fact that I had a big mailing to get out. When she saw the mailing piled on our kitchen counter, she said, "I could help you with that." After lunch, I installed her at the table with boxes of envelopes, a stack of letters, a stack of labels, and a roll of stamps. While I worked in my office, she completely got out the mailing. I will never forget the pride in her face when she finished. "I did a good job," she boasted. After that, I often called her when I had a mailing to do, and she always seemed pleased.

Delegation has two drawbacks, however. First, we can only delegate something to somebody who understands what needs to be done, so we have to explain carefully. That may take time, but is worth it if the time we spend explaining is less than the time we would spend doing it ourselves.

The second, more subtle, drawback to delegating is that we hand something over to someone else and no longer control it. Fortunately, as we begin to take more control of our lives and bring them in line with God's call and our own dreams, we need less and less to control other people and situations. When Dave Thomas, founder of Wendy's, died in 2002, his board of directors praised him because he didn't interfere with the company's daily operations. "All he wanted were regular updates on sales, profits and company goals."* Busy working to accomplish a dream, helping children get adopted, Dave Thomas could turn control even of his own corporation over to others.

Learn the ABCs

Once we've mastered the 3-Ds, the *ABCs* are easy. They are the remaining items on our to-do lists, the ones we can't drop, delay, or delegate. *A's* are the items we most value, *B's* are less valued, and *C's* are both things we do not value and things we could postpone almost indefinitely—and sometimes have. Faced with a to-do list, which do we do first?

Let's admit it—most of us think if we do the *C's* first we'll get the piddlies out of the way, then have the rest of the day to devote to *A's*. What happens? *C's* breed faster than rabbits. If we let them, they fill up our time and we piddle our days away. Do you know what happens if we ignore a *C*? It either dies a natural death or grows up to become an *A*. Consider, for instance, mopping the floor. On an ordinary Tuesday that may be a *C*, but if guests are coming for dinner . . .

Do the A's first. That's it. Do the *A's* first. And if an *A* is an event that doesn't happen until later in the day, don't wear

---

Miami Herald, January 19, 2002, 3C.

yourself out on *C's* before you get to the *A*. If an *A* truly is something you value, it deserves to be treated that way.

Coordinate Calendars

This is so simple I am embarrassed to mention it, but I find that few households or offices do it. I even find women who don't put work events on their home calendars and vice versa, which means they are constantly finding their home and office competing for their time. Be sure your house and office calendars are identical. Women who use palm pilots tell me they do a great job of synchronizing home and work calendars. Once a week or so, sit everybody in your household down to coordinate calendars. That way you will all know where stress points are, where the easy times will be, and who will be doing what.

> ✺
> **A WISE WOMAN KNOWS**
> *We get eighty percent of the value from twenty percent of what we do.*

Learn the 80/20 Rule

Business has discovered this amazing truth:

- in any organization, 80% of the work is done by 20% of the people;
- 80% of all valuable work is done in 20% of the time;
- 80% of sales are generated by 20% of sales calls;
- 80% of the work is from 20% of the files.

Similarly, in our own lives,

- 80% of the value of any phone call happens in 20% of the time;

- 80% of significant relationships are with 20% of the people we know;
- 80% of our satisfaction and accomplishment comes from 20% of our effort.

As we look at a to-do list of ten items, completing two of them will generally provide us with more satisfaction and sense of accomplishment than the other eight combined. If we identify those two and do them, it won't matter much whether we get the other eight done or not.

Let Me Say It Again

Living out our goals toward the things we truly feel called to do takes effort on our part. It requires intentional living.

We have to discard old habits, reorder our commitments, reduce the amount of time we spend on mundane tasks, and take authority over our days.

We do all this because we know that the end result is better than where we were formerly headed.

In the verse at the beginning of this section, Nehemiah tells the Israelites who have returned to Jerusalem, "The joy of the Lord is your strength." I used to think that meant that my joy in God would generate enough energy to get me through a day. Then I studied Hebrew, and discovered that the verse is talking not about my joy, but about God's joy. Literally it means "God's joy [in you] is what makes you strong."

In the movie *Chariots of Fire,* Eric Liddell is a young seminary student in Scotland studying to rejoin his parents as a missionary to China. But he is such a good runner that he has also been asked to train to represent Great Britain in the Olympic Games. When his sister chides him for putting running ahead of God, he assures her he will continue to study after the Games are over, then he explains why he must compete first. "God made me fast. I feel His pleasure when I run."

May you feel God's pleasure as you travel daily toward the goals God has set before you.

chapter twelve

Watch Out for Sabotage!

If we truly want to reduce our stress, we have to change the way we deal with saboteurs that waste our time. These saboteurs eat up our lives unless we take steps to control them.

"TIME SAVING" TECHNOLOGY

Obviously none of us would want to do without technology like microwaves and computers; but have you kept track of how much time you spend in a day simply waiting for the computer to boot, the microwave to heat something that takes a minute or less, voice mails to tell you which buttons to push (giving numerous options you do not want), e-mail to load and send messages, computer programs to run, the printer to warm up, and your own voice mail to repeat its message before it gives you your calls?

No wonder most of us feel more stressed, not less. Our lives are being subtly sucked up in snippets by "time saving" technology. But we can use waiting time to

- memorize Bible verses,
- breathe deeply,

- browse through catalogs,
- sort mail,
- tidy a desk,
- pray for someone,
- sew on a button or repair a short seam,
- take a mental mini-vacation to someplace we'd rather be,
- "Picture a Perfect You," or
- smile—our faces need the exercise.

E-Mail and Web Browsing

What is it about e-mail that seems to impose an obligation on us to frequently check it and answer right away? E-mail and the Internet gulp up enormous amounts of time. They are convenient only when we take charge of how much time they consume by

- reading e-mail only once a day;
- answering only messages that require a reply, deleting others, and separating out junk mail if that option is available;
- asking friends not to forward cute sayings, jokes, and other trivia unless they are exceptional, and doing the same ourselves; and
- keeping magazines or catalogs by the computer to browse through while waiting for Internet sites to load.

Television

Americans on the average watch four hours of television a night. That's twenty-eight hours—more than one day—a week. Turning off television can add more than fifty-two days to your year.

Telephones

Cell phones, call waiting, and voice mail options can reduce stress or cause more. Obviously cell phones provide access to help in time of danger and convenience when we need to reach someone right away. On the other hand, how often have you waited for somebody to take a call during your conversation? Similarly, call waiting allows some people to take two messages at once, but stresses people who have to wait while they take the other call. Voice messages mean we never ever miss a call. Is that a good thing? Does it reduce our stress?

There's a story of an old Vermonter whose children insisted he put in a telephone for his own convenience. One day when they were visiting, it rang and rang, but he didn't answer. When they asked why, he replied, "Right now ain't convenient."

He'd learned the secret of telephones: take control over them instead of letting them control us.

- Turn off the ringer when you are napping, enjoying a family time, or working on a project.
- When your family goes out for fun, only turn on the cell phone for an emergency.
- 10 calls x 6 minutes each = 60 minutes on the phone. How many calls do you need to make or take today?
- When somebody calls and you are busy, tell them honestly that it is not a good time to talk and suggest a time for one of you to call back.
- When you call others, make it a habit to ask if it is a good time to talk.
- If you habitually talk too long, set a timer.
- Keep a book or handwork near the phone for times you are placed on hold.

- When called by a solicitor, interrupt gently as soon as they introduce themselves and tell them you are not interested, thank them, and hang up. Don't waste your time or theirs listening to their spiel.

Meetings

There are meetings with a purpose and meetings with little purpose other than to meet. We can streamline the former and avoid the latter. To streamline meetings:

- Define clearly the tasks a meeting is to accomplish and *do major agenda items first.*
- Save items like approval of minutes and subcommittee reports until the end. You may be amazed how much less time they take when everybody's ready to leave.
- Set a time limit for a meeting and stick with it.
- Honestly budget enough time for important agenda items.
- Provide all reports and minutes ahead of time and send via e-mail or snail mail. Presume people will read them. If they don't, that's their problem.
- Take time early in the meeting for each person to briefly share important events or issues in their lives. This will cut down on chatter later.
- Never attempt to edit in the whole committee. Appoint an editing committee.
- Replace meetings with a conference call whenever possible.

Clutter

Clutter kills. It increases stress, which aggravates heart problems and can lead ultimately to death. Think about that as you read this section and look about your home. Pick up a few extraneous items in your home and ask, "Is this worth dying for?" Another way to ask the question is, "Does this have meaning in my life?"

Clutter is too much of anything for the space we have. It is magazines and newspapers we don't read, clothes we don't wear, dishes we don't eat on, cookbooks we never open, papers we will never use, books we will never read again, files we don't open, mementos we don't even like, and appliances that no longer work.

A WISE PERSON ONCE SAID

"The coat hanging unused in your closet belongs to one who needs it; the shoes rotting in your closet belong to the person who has no shoes."
–Basil the Great of Caesarea, ca. 365

Clutter is probably the most subtle saboteur in our lives. We scarcely notice how much time we spend moving unused items to reach ones we need. But clutter wastes our life whenever we dust it, pack and pay to move it, shuffle through clothes we don't wear seeking those we do, shift a mug we don't use to reach one we do, or pick up papers and put them down again. Here are some ways to deal with clutter.

- Consider your clothes, dishes, books, blankets, pillows, CDs and tapes, DVDs and videos, furniture, tools, and electrical appliances. Which have you not used in the past two years? Chances are that you won't use those things again. If you did, could you borrow, rent, or buy one temporarily? Give unneeded items away.
- Ask, "How many of each thing do I need, how many do I want, and how many do I have?" If you have more than you either need or want, give some away.

- Each time you buy a new book, blouse, CD, or pair of shoes, give one away.
- When something breaks and you don't repair it within a year, discard it.
- Take magazines and books to a nursing home, homeless shelter, or other place where people might like to read them.
- For holidays and birthdays, give friends and family members things of your own they have admired.
- For holidays and birthdays, repair broken items rather than buying new ones.
- Hold a garage sale and donate the proceeds to a charity.
- If clutter is necessary—and sometimes it is, when you are working on a project—set up a card table in an unused corner to contain it. Maxine's husband built her several decorative screens to put around cluttered tables holding projects.
- For necessary clutter, consider adding shelves to closets, bookshelves above doorways, another closet, or a storage shed. Beware, though—one woman bought lots of storage boxes to hold her sewing and crafts clutter. So far the boxes, unfilled, are stacked in a corner of her bedroom, increasing her clutter.

Procrastination

Procrastination is a habit that greatly increases stress. We are constantly behind, trying to play catch-up with our lives.

Beth spoke of why she used to habitually procrastinate. "I lived with the false belief that anything worth doing had to be done perfectly. Writing a letter, for instance, could take me hours, because I wanted it to be exactly right. So I'd put off writing letters. Then God showed me Isaiah 28:15, 'For we have made a lie our refuge and falsehood our hiding place.' I saw that I was living a lie. Nobody expected perfection of me, just a willingness to try. People needed a note from me, not a perfect epistle."

Why do we procrastinate?

- A task looks hard.
- We want to do something perfectly.
- We're scared we can't do it at all.
- We fear if we succeed, we may be asked to do bigger things.*
- A task looks unpleasant.

If you are a habitual procrastinator—or if you don't habitually procrastinate, but there's something you keep putting off—consider why you are avoiding a specific task.

- Is it too difficult? Look for one or two easy pieces to begin with.
- Is it unpleasant? What unpleasantness will it entail? How bad is it really likely to be? Sometimes our dread of something is worse than the thing itself. How long will the unpleasantness last? How quickly could you do it if you don't do it perfectly, but merely competently?
- Are you afraid you will fail? What is the worst that could happen if you do? Let yourself picture that, then think what you will do if that worst scenario does happen. Once you have planned how to deal with the very worst, you can get on with the job.

---

*Studies have shown that some women are extremely reluctant to succeed.

- What is the best thing that could happen? List possible positive outcomes and post them where you can see them as you work.

Once you have identified why you are procrastinating, here are tips for getting on with the task:

- Prayerfully consider who else could help you with this. Working with another on big projects can energize you both.
- Break large, difficult tasks into smaller, manageable ones.
- Do hard or unpleasant tasks when you are fresh or rested.
- Promise yourself a specific reward when you have completed a certain part of the task. (I talk more about rewarding yourself in chapter 14.)
- For projects with a deadline—a visit to the dentist, elective surgery, making a speech—remind yourself that it will be over by a certain time. Focus your attention on that time.
- Make a deal with yourself to work for a certain amount of time and set a timer. Quit when the time is up.

If all else fails and you are still procrastinating, give up. Admit you don't want to do this thing—maybe you aren't even supposed to be doing this thing. Confess to anyone you need to, then get on with your life. Sometimes we take on tasks for which we are neither suited nor inclined.

 What saboteurs currently consume too much of my time? How will I change that?

THE DANGER OF TOO-EFFICIENT LIVING

We have already heard how Beth saw that a desire to be perfect gets in the way of being human. It increases our stress. We can live so efficiently we sabotage our efforts to live *effectively*. People are important. It's important, therefore, to take time for play as well as work, for leisure as well as activity. Sometimes we accomplish the most by doing nothing! Breakfast dates with a friend or spouse, games with children, celebrations with coworkers, parties for a congregation—these are life builders, not time wasters.

Rabbi Abraham J. Heschel wrote what could be a goal for us all: "What I look for is not how to gain a firm hold on myself and on life, but primarily how to live a life that would deserve and invoke an eternal Amen."[*]

We will talk more about that kind of life in chapter 14. First, I'll give you a few tips that can save time each day for things you most want to do.

---

[*]Abraham Joshua Heschel, *The Wisdom of Heschel*, selected by Ruth Marcus Goodhill (New York: Farrar, Straus and Giroux, 1975), 3.

chapter thirteen

Tips to Make Life Easier

I once saw a lovely Chinese dance in which each dancer held four or five bamboo rods. A china plate was balanced on top of each rod, and as the women danced, each plate twirled merrily. The women lowered the rods, raised the rods, even switched rods from hand to hand. I couldn't help thinking that they were performing the Dance of a Woman's Life.

Daily we balance people, priorities, and possibilities. On good days, they all keep twirling overhead. Some days, they get overbalanced and crash around us.

A skillful dancer knows how many rods she can keep twirling at the same time. A wise woman knows how many balls of life she can juggle in a day or a season of her life. She also knows which things have to be done really well, and which can be done less well and still achieve adequate results.

However, even when we are doing what most energizes us, what we know we want to do and feel we were created to be doing, life can get hectic and too full. Here are suggestions that can help reduce stress and simplify life a bit. Choose the ones that can make life easier for you.

THE 80/20 RULE REVISITED

CLEANING TIPS FROM A WISE MAID
If it doesn't look dirty, don't clean it. If you do the floors and make the beds, the house looks clean. You will always clean longest in the room you begin in, so start in the dirtiest room.

In our homes, this principle suggests that:

- we use 20% of our recipes 80% of the time;
- we use 20% of our dishes 80% of the time;
- we wear 20% of our clothes 80% of the time.
- 20% of our houses get 80% of the dirt.

If we copy recipes we use most often and put them together in one place, we don't waste time thumbing through cookbooks. If we put dishes we don't use on upper shelves, we don't have to shift them to get dishes we want. If we put clothes we wear in the most convenient part of our closets, we don't waste time rummaging through unworn ones to find them. If we clean the dirtiest part of the house, the house will look clean.

 How could I use the 80/20 rule to simplify my own life?

DIRECTORIES AND FILES

- List all doctors under "D," all babysitters under "B," etc., to save time trying to remember names or looking up separate numbers.

- Keep rosters for all groups you belong to in one file or looseleaf notebook.
- If you have a lot of appointments in a year, label a file folder for each month. File all information about engagements under the month in which the event will happen, rather than making files for one-time events.
- Make a hard copy of your e-mail address book to avoid losing it. Print out a new copy every month or two.
- Income tax time isn't a hassle if you keep all important receipts, paid bills, canceled checks, and expense accounts in one box or big brown envelope.
- Staple the receipt for any major purchase to the product information booklet, and keep all warranties and product information booklets in one file.
- When changing a friend's address or phone number in your personal or computer address book, note the date you changed it. You won't wonder later if that's the new address.
- Make one file listing all bank accounts, stock accounts, insurance policies, and investments.
- Keep children's test scores, vaccination records, etc., in one file.

ENTERTAINING

- If others bring food to your parties, they feel it's their party too. Some of our most successful parties have been "Bring your own meat to grill and one dish to share." Maxine points out, "The purpose of a party is to have fun, not show off."
- For your birthday or Christmas, ask for candlesticks, tablecloths, centerpieces, or a box of pretty paper napkins

to use when you entertain. Buy candles and pretty napkins when you see them on sale. Keep plastic eating utensils, cups, and paper plates on hand, so you can put together a party at short notice.

- Make-your-own party foods are easy and fun: baked potatoes with a variety of toppings, salad items set out in a salad bar, two or three ice creams with several toppings.
- Ice cream cones are a big hit and a breeze to organize for preschool and elementary school birthday parties, especially if the teacher will let the class eat outdoors. Take your scoop and paper napkins from home, pick up ice cream and cones on your way.

ERRANDS

- Never run one errand if you can put it off. Wait until you need to do two or three.
- Have an errand basket into which you deposit everything you need for errands—shoes that need repair, library books to return, grocery coupons, letters and parcels to mail, checks to deposit. When you are ready to run errands, pick up the basket and go.
- Before you leave home, plot your errands in a geographical loop.
- Never make a trip when a phone call will do.

FLEXIBILITY

Look for a pleasant use for an unpleasant situation. When the power went out, our older son said, "What a perfect time to tell ghost stories." When a car broke down on vacation, Sandra's family enjoyed two unexpected days in a lovely campground. Mystery author Elizabeth Daniel Squire had a marvelous ability to see the positive in any situation. When we had to stand nearly an hour waiting to get into a reception, Liz pointed out, "We were going in there to stand around and talk. We can start the party out here."

HOLIDAYS AND SPECIAL EVENTS

- Buy several birthday cards and get well cards when you are near a card rack, and keep them on hand for when you need them.
- Note birthdays and anniversaries on your calendar under the day you need to mail the card or letter rather than under the day itself.
- "Make a memory" instead of buying a gift. Some birthday memories our children selected were a trip to a museum, dinner at a Japanese steak house, and a day at the county fair.
- Make your own simple family traditions. One family we know elects to spend each Thanksgiving camping instead of cooking an enormous meal. Our family serves steak, baked potatoes, and salad for Christmas dinner, so we don't have to cook very much.

MAJOR TASKS

- List everything that will need to be done a few days ahead. The act of writing it down will fix it more clearly in your mind.
- Break major tasks into smaller pieces that can be accomplished in bits and pieces of time. Post a list of "pieces" in a prominent place and check off items when finished.
- If small children or housebound adults prevent your accomplishing a major task, hire a one-time sitter while you do what you must.

- When a task requires concentration, control interruptions. Don't answer the phone. Don't make calls. Don't check e-mail. Give yourself the number of hours you need to get the task done. You may even go where you cannot be reached by phone and leave the cell phone at home. Libraries, empty church classrooms, even airport waiting rooms are good places to study or write. If necessary, arrange to use a friend's house while she is at work or away.

MAIL

- Never deal with a piece of paper twice unless you have to.
- Put a wastebasket near your front door and drop junk mail into it as you bring it into the house. Don't let junk letters and unwanted catalogs clutter your home.
- Place bills unopened in a basket until you are ready to pay them.
- Keep unanswered letters in another basket near your desk.
- Whenever possible, answer business mail by hand on the letter itself to save time and paper. Make a copy for your "pending" file if necessary.
- Pretty postcards are faster to write and cheaper to mail than letters, and just as appreciated.
- Evaluate magazines you receive and stop subscriptions to those you don't read.

MEALS

- Once a week or so, have a "microwave buffet" for which you spread out all the week's leftovers, let each family member put together his or her own meal, and microwave each plate. Add fruit or a salad to perk up the leftovers.

- Grocers count on the fact that one-fourth of each shopping cart is filled with impulse items. Save time and money by shopping less often.

- School-age children can fix simple meals. Let them choose the menu, make sure the ingredients are there, and let them do it once a week.

- Start a loose-leaf notebook for each child containing recipes for his or her favorite foods. Children (and husbands) are more likely to learn to cook what they like to eat.

A WISE WOMAN KNOWS
She who clips another recipe when she has a hundred untried ones is wasting time.

- Collect recipes you use most often in a loose-leaf folder or photo album. Use dividers for various categories. Put into that folder *only* recipes you use frequently.

SPACES YOU INHABIT

- Designate one drawer the "junk" drawer and don't feel guilty for needing it.

- Put items you use most often in the most accessible places and those you use less often toward the back. Move clothes you wear toward the front of your closets, dishes you use to your most accessible shelves. If you are older or live alone, put two of all items in easy reach and move the rest up higher. Store heavy items like casserole dishes down low where you can reach them more easily.

- Analyze your use of shelves and drawers, both at home and at work. Are utensils you use at the sink near the sink and those you use at the stove near the stove? At work, are supplies you use most often the easiest to reach?
- Teach children four and older to put away their own clothes. For young ones, tape a picture to each drawer showing what goes in that drawer.
- Use rooms for your own purposes. A single man put his billiard table in the dining room and ate on a snack tray in his den. Miriam's family uses their living room as a computer room/library and their "den" as the living room. Shelly's family uses what the builder designated the "breakfast room" as a play room for the children.

When a college friend called recently to say she was about to begin a writing career, she mentioned, "I write in my guest room."

"Why don't you let guests sleep in your office, instead?" I suggested.

She called later to report, "Changing the name also changed my idea about the room, and made a lot of difference in how I furnished, arranged, and decorated it."

A WISE WOMAN KNOWS
You may have to live in a crowd but you do not have to live like the crowd.

chapter fourteen

Coping in a Less than Perfect World

I once knew a young mother with a knack for wise sayings. When a family crisis interfered with her arriving at a meeting on time, she reminded us, "The world stops for dirty diapers."

Wouldn't it be great if there were no dirty diapers or their daily equivalents? If we weren't constantly having to lay aside the important to deal with the urgent? If we could make phone calls by 9 A.M. and follow a well-organized schedule with no interruptions or deviations all day?

Actually, I'm not sure that would be wonderful. An occasional bump in the road keeps a driver from falling asleep. The less-than-perfect holidays are the ones we later laugh about. That unexpected last crag is what makes the mountain climb most memorable. And no matter how much we yearn for a perfect world, we don't live in one. We live in a world where people we call aren't home or have to call us back, a world where letters we want to write require further research and have to be laid aside, where unexpected deadlines overlap with deadlines we already face. We live in a world where people with a crisis need us right that minute. We live in a world where cars break down, bikes get stolen, fillings fall out, and computers crash. Accidents happen. Loved ones drastically disappoint us. They even die. As I was working on this chapter I got a call that my friend Debra's beloved dog had been killed by a car. Instead of writing, I needed to comfort Debra and help her plan Sweetie's burial.

Therefore, since imperfect parts of the world impinge on our lives and add to our stress, every woman needs a repertoire of skills to handle days when things go wrong.

TAKE TIME TO BE HOLY

Women who cope well with stress all seem to have one thing in common: they are grounded in holiness. That doesn't mean they are sickeningly pious, but rather that they daily take time not just for quick Bible reading or prayer on the run, they actually sit down in silence to listen to and reflect on God and God's word. As Betty said, "Devotional times frame my life and give structure to it."

The idea of taking time out of our busy days for prayer, Scripture and devotional reading may sound like adding just one more thing to an already crammed schedule. Actually, time for holiness is a stop by the filling station of your soul before your empty car coasts to stop.

Marilyn reported, "I found my attitude toward prayer and Bible study changed when I decided that one of my personal life goals would be to deepen my relationship with God through regular devotions. I started putting Bible study and prayer on each month's goal list, and have discovered that now those times have become not 'have to's' but 'want and need to's' in my life."

Beginning may seem daunting, if you haven't had a habit of prayer and study. Here are a few tips that might help you get started.

- *Buy a Bible that attracts you.* That means one that is easy for you to hold, one with type that entices you to read, one with margins for notes if you are a note taker, one whose pages will take underlining if you like to underline. A new Bible can be exciting because the Word of God seems new and fresh.

- *Establish a "holy place" in your home.* This is a place where it is easy for you to sit, study, and pray. It may be a special chair or one end of the couch. It can even be a basket to hold your Bible, notebook, pen, and devotional reading, which you carry from place to place. Be sure you have a place for a cup if you like to sip coffee or tea while you read. You might want a nearby CD player for devotional music.

- *Don't start reading the Bible at the beginning and try to read through.* The Bible isn't a book, it's a collection of books, a spiritual cafeteria. As you begin, thumb through or read the Table of Contents until something catches your eye, and you find yourself thinking, "Hmm ... I haven't ever read that particular book in the Bible," or, "I remember hearing a verse from this book not long ago, and thinking that someday I'd like to read the whole thing," or even, "I like the name of that book. I think I'll read it next." I find it helpful as I finish reading a book to note my completion date in the Table of Contents to keep track of how recently I've read it.

- *Collect some aids to holy living: devotional books, perhaps a prayer journal, CDs or tapes that can quiet your soul and open it up to God.* Some people like to journal during their devotions. Others write their prayers, so they can remember what they have asked for and make notes of answers. Others use a CD devotionally instead of forming word-prayers. Try praying by just picturing yourself in the throne room of God, bowed in awe.

- *Spend as much time in silence and prayer as you spend in reading.*

- *Keep a prayer notebook where you jot down things you want to remember to pray about or people you want to pray for.* Cross them off or jot a date when a prayer is answered.

Beth—mother of four and a seminary professor's wife— spoke of taking "prayer breaks" in her busy life. "I'd go to my room and sit in my favorite chair until I sensed the presence of God. Those times got me through many a day. Sometimes when I got particularly crabby, the children would beg, 'Mama, go take a prayer break.'"

Your own prayer break can come in the morning, during children's naps, during your lunch break, before bed—any time that works for your schedule. But lives are far less stressful when they are framed by prayer.

REMEMBER THE SABBATH

Remember the Sabbath? That's the day of rest we are told to take once a week. One day of rest a week is so important to our bodies, our spirits, and our minds that God devoted one-tenth of the commandments to "Remember the Sabbath, to keep it holy." Yet perfectly nice folks, who would never consider stealing, committing adultery, or murdering somebody, treat Sunday (or Saturday, for some) like just another day of the week to do laundry, dishes, cooking, and catch up on all the work they've brought home from the office. No wonder we're all so exhausted.

If we look at how Jesus observed the Sabbath, it was a day for bringing *shalom*—peace, health, holiness, comfort, and even salvation—into the world. God, after creating the universe, simply "rested." The point seems to be that we are not to run at full-speed seven days a week, we are to take one day a week to refresh our spirit, mind, and body and spread *shalom* in the world.

Imagine if somebody came up to you and said, "Here is an extra day for you to sit and look at the surface of a lake, take a long nap, lie in the grass with a child blowing dandelion heads, visit with a friend you don't often have time with, read some of those books you have stacked beside your bed, play the piano, write that note you've been wanting to write, or just stare into space." Wouldn't you be delighted? Well, God gives you that gift every single week.

Try this experiment. For one month, resolve that no matter how busy you are, you will stop work at sundown one day and not resume until sundown the next. If Saturday evening to Sunday evening works for you, great. But if not, choose one day that is your own "Sabbath."

- Cook a big meal the night before so you can eat planned-overs the next day.
- Deliberately do *not* turn on the computer, go to the office, or do a lick of housework or yard work except for tasks that refresh you.

- Declare a homework Sabbath, as well.
- Make plans for how you want to spend the time. Playing games? Watching golf on television (now, there is a slow-down idea)? Reading? Visiting a park? Putting photos in albums? Taking a long nap? Or . . . ?
- If this is your regular day of worship, worship, but don't attend any meetings afterwards.
- Evaluate after the month. Did you still get as much work done as you did before? Do you feel more refreshed?

I suspect you'll find yourself more productive the other six days, and will get through hard parts of the week looking forward to your day of rest. My husband and I declared ourselves Sabbath observers several years ago. We've been amazed at what that does to the rest of the week.

TRUST GOD IN THE MEANTIME

What do we do when we are doing something we feel God wants us to do, and something else very important interrupts that we suspect God also wants us to do? We stay calm and trust God in the meantime. Jesus taught this lesson by his actions in the story that begins at Luke 8:40.

On his way to heal a dying child—a situation that greatly stressed the father and the disciples—Jesus was surrounded by a jostling crowd. In that crowd was a woman who for twelve years had had menstrual bleeding that exhausted her body and her pocketbook. Desperate for healing, she didn't bother Jesus, just sneaked up to touch his robe. However, he sensed that she was there.

What would you have done if you were Jesus at that point? Pretend the interruption hadn't happened? Dealt with it quickly in order to get on with the "important," God-given mission?

Jesus stopped. He looked around and asked, "Who touched me?"

How frantic the father and that crowd must have become. Luke records the stress of Peter in his impatience as he points out the obvious. "Lord, the people are crowding and pressing against you."

Jesus wasn't stressed. Perfectly relaxed, he stopped and scanned the crowd. "No, I felt the power go out of me. Who touched me?" He waited. The crowd fumed, knowing the child was growing worse, but Jesus waited until the woman crept forward to confess. Then he spoke gentle words of comfort: "Daughter, your faith has healed you. Go in peace." After that, he peacefully headed toward his original destination.

How did he avoid getting stressed by that kind of interruption? I think Jesus spent his life discerning what it was that God wanted him to do each minute. He was so focused on God that he could discern when an interruption came from God. And he knew an important truth about doing God's will: *If God sends an interruption in the middle of another assignment, God will take care of the first assignment in the meantime, while we deal with the interruption.*

I have been testing that principle for years, and I can tell you with confidence, it works. The first test I made was one summer when I was teaching at one conference center and my husband was teaching at one forty minutes away. He asked me to dinner to meet a special friend, but just as I was about to leave, a woman stopped me in obvious pain. What should I do? Those were the days before cell phones, so I couldn't reach Bob. But the woman's need to talk to somebody was visible. I had just studied that story in Luke, so for the first time in my life I winged a prayer: "Lord, I'm stopping here, believing it's your will. If so, please don't let Bob worry until I can get there." Perfectly relaxed, I talked with the woman for over an hour.

I made an intentional decision not to speed on the way, and when I arrived for dinner very late, Bob and his friend were just arriving too. "Sorry we're late," they apologized. "We got held up in our meeting."

That one situation might have been a fluke, but it's happened often enough since for me to know intellectually that when I listen for God's direction in my schedule, I can move at a leisurely pace and still accomplish all I truly need to do—sometimes far more. If I'm going to a meeting and hit every red light on the way, I am no longer astonished to arrive and find nobody else got there on time either. If I have a deadline and somebody calls with an urgent need to talk or come over, I actually wait to see how God is going to help with the deadline. Each time this happens I find myself delighted at how relaxed God makes life at times.

However, I still have trouble living out what I know. I know that some interruptions are not sent for me to deal with, but to test my commitment to what I was called to do. I also know that I am prone to be like that crowd: fixing my eye on the long-range task, resenting interruptions and impatient with delays. Life, I find, is a constant lesson in trying to discern

- when to diligently keep on working and when to stop and spend time with somebody who wants or needs my attention,
- when to talk longer on the phone and when to cut it short,

- when to insist on time to be alone and when to visit with somebody else,
- when to drive on and when to stop to help another traveler.

Right now, as I juggle writing this book, selling our home, and getting accustomed to having my mother-in-law live with us, it is a great time to work on daily listening, to practice trying to discern when an interruption needs to be dealt with right then and when I can delay a request and forge on with writing. I haven't perfected the art yet, but I'm trying. And I promise you this: If God gives you an important job to do, then sends an important interruption on the way, you don't need to get stressed by the interruption. Deal with it. God will take care of your original destination in the meantime.

CALL A FRIEND

It's a proven fact: a chat, lunch, or a quick cup of coffee with a friend actually reduces a woman's stress.

A UCLA study, reported by the *Penn State News Wire* service in August, 2000, looked at differences between the male and female response to stress. The research team, headed by Dr. Shelley E. Taylor, discovered that whereas a man's response to stress is most likely either fight or flight, we women in times of stress tend to take care of children or seek out other women. There's a chemical reason for this. The team studied the cascade of chemicals released in the brain in response to stress, particularly the hormone oxytocin, a mood regulator. They found that in women, the release of oxytocin buffers the flight or fight response and triggers either a desire to tend children or what the scientists called "a friend seeking response." They found that estrogen seems to enhance the effects of oxytocin, while testosterone seems to reduce its effect. Furthermore, when we women respond to stress by tending to children or seeking out a friend, the study suggests that more oxytocin is released, which additionally counters our stress and calms us even more.

Team member Laura Cousino Klein says, "This doesn't mean that women never become angry or aggressive, or that men never tend or befriend, but the 'tend and befriend' response to stress is more common among women."[*]

So the next time you are overwhelmed and feel a need to spend time with a child or call a friend, listen to the urge. It's your God-given response to stress.

REMEMBER: YOUR BODY *IS* YOUR SELF

Sometimes we act like we are disembodied spirits. We forget that stress takes a toll on our bodies and weary, overworked bodies contribute to our stress. Here are some simple but very powerful physical stress relievers:

- Eat right. Be sure you get enough vitamins.
- Get enough sleep. Studies show that we get our deepest, best sleep before midnight, so going to bed earlier can reduce stress.
- Nap. Many women with low stress levels mention naps as one coping mechanism. Even half an hour can refresh you. And don't tell me your preschoolers won't nap. Children can be taught to nap just as they are taught to eat three times a day or use a toilet. Day care centers schedule a nap into every afternoon. You can too.

---

[*]Internet news release of PennStateNewsWire/Science, August 30, 2000.

- Relax. Set a timer and lie flat on your back with your arms beside you. Breath deeply and, beginning with your toes, relax each muscle in your body. Picture stress flowing out of your toes, drawn into the earth by gravity. Five minutes of this can be as good as a half-hour nap.
- Breathe deeply. Exhale. Then fill your lungs with all the air they can hold. Retain while you count to five. Exhale all the air you can force from your lungs. Repeat four times.
- Take a long bath by candlelight.
- Treat yourself to a professional massage.
- Give yourself five minutes in your favorite outdoor space doing absolutely nothing except enjoying the view and the fresh air.
- Exercise: take a walk, go for a run, swim, do aerobics.

ACCEPT YOUR LIMITATIONS

Most of the time when we think we have too much to do, it's because we truly have too much to do. However, much of our stress comes not from other people's expectations but from our own high expectations and from trying to live up to what we *think* others expect of us. Yet, just as the world is not perfect, we are not perfect. We can eliminate a good bit of stress by accepting who we are and what we can realistically do. Avoid spreading yourself too thin. Maxine gave us a good example when she said, "I don't accept jobs I can't do well."

When you have overestimated your own abilities—have taken on more than you can do in the allotted time—jettison! That means, throw overboard everything you absolutely do not have to do, anything you can postpone, and anything you can pass on to others. Then consider what must be done well, what can be done less well, and what can be done poorly and still count. There are times when it is appropriate to sweep dirt under the rug.

There are also times when it is appropriate to ask for help. As we prepared for this move, we had many special friends in Miami we wanted to spend time with before we left. In order to get our books and dishes packed and still have time for friends, I decided to combine the two. We held two "goodbye" parties and asked each guest to pack one box as we laughed and talked together. At the suggestion of one friend, I printed up some labels: "Packed by the loving hands of..." and each person signed the box she packed. Some added a little message. In our new home, we will have the fun of remembering each of them as we shelve books and unpack dishes.

ADMIT WHAT A MARVEL YOU ARE

Under enormous pressure, we women perform Herculean tasks. Then, we are prone to collapse into a chair, worn to the bone, and think of five more things we ought to be doing or haven't done. Ann suggests that instead, we take time to bask in what marvels we are.

"I remember when one of my preschool daughters had strep throat at the same time the other had bronchitis. Since both were diabetics, their differing schedules of antibiotics and other medicines were added to an already full schedule of two insulin shots, six to eight urine tests and six meals each per day. I was feeling pretty exhausted and depressed until one night I counted up and realized I had done *forty* specific scheduled things in that one day. I sat down, put my feet up, and knew I had earned a rest. I had done everything I was supposed to do, which was a lot. I was a real hero."

A manual for caregivers of the chronically ill, disabled, or aged suggests that when they are feeling weary and overwhelmed, they should list people who have told them recently that they are doing a good job, and then *believe them*. I think this applies to any woman who has put out incredible effort and accomplished a big task: mothers of newborns and mothers of brides; women who meet difficult deadlines and women who complete a degree; parents of sick children and children of sick parents; women who run church bazaars and Christmas pageants; women who plan and conduct Easter music; women who stand on their feet all day teaching children—you know who you are and what you have done. When you've been under a lot of stress and come through it victorious, pat yourself on the back. You are a blooming marvel!

GIVE YOURSELF PERMISSION

Gloria, a Christian counselor, advises that we women may need to give ourselves permission to become and do what we want to become and do. To alleviate stress in our lives, we need to give ourselves permission to

- follow our dreams and abilities. Achieve what we can achieve.
- ask for help or advice when we need them, and refuse them when we don't.
- be angry with others who expect too much from us. Depression is often anger turned inward. How many women are depressed because they turn legitimate anger at somebody else inward toward themselves?
- be angry with God when life is awful. God can take our anger.

- say no.
- cry.
- feel scared.
- feel brave.
- grow and change.

 Is there something I need to give myself permission to do?

REWARD YOURSELF

Several women I interviewed explained how they reward themselves for hard work accomplished in stressful situations. When Donna has to prepare a speech for an international conference, she promises herself that as soon as the speech is written, she'll buy herself a nice outfit to present it in. As a lawyer who helps elderly people plan their estates, Elise spends most of her time in her car; her reward is a comfortable one she enjoys driving. Shirley goes fishing. Maxine drives to another town and walks around the stores. Priscilla takes bubble baths by candlelight. I go to bed early with a mystery. Call it a reward or a celebration, one way to reduce stress in our lives is to balance work with rewards that are special for us. (I received an e-mail as I was writing this chapter telling me to remember what stressed is spelled backwards.)

Discover Mini-Vacations

One special way to reward yourself is to take a mini-vacation—a brief time away from daily stress. Mini-vacations can last a minute or a few hours. The week before a wedding, spend an hour in a park. The week of a deadline, quit early one night and rent a movie. I take a weekly mini-vacation while my mother-in-law gets her hair fixed—I spend an hour with a friend. Not long ago when I had a speaking engagement in Lake Wales, Florida, I added two hours to my trip to wander through the Bok Tower botanical gardens. That time in the dew-fresh morning still makes me take a deep relaxed breath whenever I think of it.

Everybody needs mini-vacations. I recommend a brief one at least once a day. During weeks of greatest stress, plan in a few hours when you can be refreshed. Let these suggestions spark your imagination and generate ideas of your own. The important thing is to intentionally *relax* during the vacation.

- Sit down in a comfortable chair and listen to your favorite music without doing anything else. How long has it been since you really listened to a piece of music?
- Visit a local art museum, sit down, and truly enjoy one painting.
- Visit a local historical site or park.
- Take off your shoes and walk barefoot in the grass.
- Close your eyes, bury your nose in a fragrant flower, and breathe deeply.
- Meet a friend in the middle of the afternoon for ice cream or dessert at a restaurant where you generally pass up the desserts because meals are so large.
- Carry a chair to a pretty part of your property and sit there for a few minutes to enjoy it.
- Take a small child for a short walk.
- Close your eyes and spend a few imaginary minutes in your favorite place on earth.

- Call somebody you like and haven't chatted with for some time.
- Go online to webshots.com and create computer wallpaper and screen savers using photos from places you'd like to see. Occasionally stop working and let yourself enter one of those pictures. In one day you can pause to feel autumn breezes on the Great Wall of China, listen to the roar of Victoria Falls, feel the chill of snow surrounding a Scottish castle, stand beside the Namibian Desert at dawn, and sit on a Caribbean beach.
- Plant a flower or two.
- Rent a movie you used to love and haven't seen for a while, or a classic you missed.
- Audit a class in a subject you like or want to know something about.
- Volunteer one hour a week in a program very different from what you normally do.
- Take time again to picture the perfect you.

Mini-vacations can be almost as restful as longer ones.

IN ALL THINGS GIVE THANKS

I used to be surprised and amazed at how often the words "thanks" and "thankful" flow from the lips of women who have overcome stress in their lives. Now I realize that what Bonnie calls her "attitude of gratitude" in some inexplicable way generates energy for living.

She explained, "When I am particularly stressed, I find myself thanking God for little things I usually take for granted—flush toilets, a pillow beneath my head, carpets on my floor, running water. As I thank God for these blessings, others come to mind. I spent one week praising God for my ancestors. I find that when I make a deliberate effort to be grateful rather than to complain, stress begins to unravel."

The most thankful woman I know is Betty's mother and my own dear friend. The fall before I revised this book, she celebrated her 102nd birthday and informed me she has voted in every national election since women were given the vote. In her extraordinarily long life she has known sickness, stress, and sorrow, yet she bubbles with gratitude and praise. To be in her presence is to feel you have blessed her by your very existence. To hear her constant gratitude reminds me of blessings I'd forgotten. Betty says, "Mother is a living example that order springs out of a life of giving thanks to God. Thanksgiving transforms daily chores and menial tasks that otherwise can be drab and boring. Truly, if there is one thing Mother has given the world, it is an example of a thankful heart."

WOMEN WHO DO JUST ENOUGH

In a French chateau, I once stood before a gorgeous tapestry depicting a medieval hunting scene. I marveled at the hours of planning and execution that went into creating that masterpiece, and tears ran down my cheeks as I realized that while painters' names are written on their masterpieces, the names of the women who created that tapestry are lost to history.

Fortunately our own names are written on the hand of God, the Divine Weaver, who plans a tapestry for each of us. A truly wise woman seeks God's priorities for each day and focuses on those, trusting the Weaver to fit each day into the total tapestry of her life.

I hope this book will be of help to you as you seek God's plan for your own life tapestry. Stretch your horizons toward your dreams and clear out other things cluttering your life and your soul. Remember:

> God doesn't want you busy about everything.
> However, God does want you busy about some things.
> If you listen, God will tell you what they are.

Let Your Dream Grow Within You

> *Delight yourself in the Lord and he will give you the desires of your heart.*
>
> —Psalm 37:4

As I said in chapter 7, God not so much grants our desires as plants them within our hearts. God gives the desires themselves. And the Divine Weaver has a plan for how those dreams fit not only into the total tapestry of our own lives, but into the tapestry that is the Kingdom of God.

TRY THIS EXERCISE

Sit quietly before the throne of God. Delight yourself in the Lord. Think of wonderful, fun things God has put in your path during your lifetime—things you have seen, special places you have been, people you have met, unexpected surprises that delighted you. Look out the window at the wonderful day God has given you. Feel God's love pouring over you like warm golden light. Breathe deeply of that light. Bask in it.

Now picture God planting a dream within you in a shaft of light. First, it is only a quiver in the darkness within you.

Open yourself to an image of that dream growing within you. Perhaps you will see a seed that sprouts and sends out shoots that grow toward the light that is God's love. What kind of seed is it? What does the plant look like? Smell like? Can you see it spreading to embrace you? Perhaps you will see a bit of yeast dough that expands in the warmth of God's love. Relax as it swells to fill you with its fragrance and substance. Perhaps you will see an image that is particularly your own. I see a small book that grows and grows until I myself become the book.

Whatever you see, sit quietly and let the dream God is planting within you grow until it fills every crevice of your body, soul, and spirit. Then prayerfully, say two words: "Yes, Lord."

Afterword

In the first edition of this book I described fourteen women who graciously let me interview them and whose wisdom formed much of the content of that book. For this edition I have drawn on some of their experiences, but also on stories told me by many women from workshops and retreats. Because I have no way to contact most of them for biographical information, I omit bios in this edition.

Your stories are important too. If you want to contact me, please feel free to write me in care of Zondervan, who will forward your letter. If you want to know more about my other books, check out my website, www.patriciasprinkle.com.

P.S. In case you wondered, a child in our congregation found a home for our kitten. Then at the party on our last Sunday in town, the new owners of our house informed me they had decided to keep the mama cat. Yay God!

SAMPLE GOALS WORKSHEET

Instructions: In a notebook or on the computer, create a worksheet and fill in each category after prayerful thought. Later you may want separate pages for life goals, season goals, annual goals, and monthly goals. When you update your monthly goals and annual goals, refer to your life and long-term goals to keep all goals consistent.

Remember, no goals are set in stone. They can be amended as you live with them awhile.

Date: _____

My current long-term season: From now until _____
Approximate years in this season: _____

PERSONAL GOALS (Choose categories that apply to your own life.)

Life Goal: (What do I want to become by the end of my life? What will I most regret not having been done?)

Long-Term Goal: (What do I want to be accomplished by the end of this season of my life? What will I most regret not having been done by then?)

Annual Goal(s): (What step can I take toward meeting this goal during the next 12 months or during this shorter season of my life? Can I take more than one step this year to move me toward the larger goal? What will I need to do in various months to meet my annual goal(s)?)

Month's Goal(s): (What can I realistically accomplish toward this goal in this month? The first month or two may involve planning, revisiting your budget, considering a schedule to rearrange commitments to provide time to work on the goal, or even rearranging your house to make space to work on the goal.)

PROFESSIONAL GOALS
    LIFE GOAL: _____
    Long-Term Goal: _____
    Annual Goal(s): _____
    Monthly Goal(s): _____

FAMILY GOALS
    LIFE GOAL: _____
    Long-Term Goal: _____
    Annual Goal(s): _____
    Monthly Goal(s): _____

CHURCH/COMMUNITY GOALS
    LIFE GOAL: _____
    Long-Term Goal: _____
    Annual Goal(s): _____
    Monthly Goal(s): _____

Children Who Do Too Little

Why Your Kids Need to Work Around the House (and How to Get Them to Do It)

Patricia Sprinkle

Many parents, rather than fighting their children over chores, would rather do the chores themselves. But Patricia Sprinkle argues convincingly and entertainingly that kids need to do chores. They need to develop basic life skills such as cooking and cleaning. They need to learn responsibility and the value of hard work. In short, they need to learn how to become dependable, capable adults.

In *Children Who Do Too Little,* Sprinkle shows why and how parents should teach their children household skills and gives suggestions for making teaching easier. She discusses

- Why we do it all for our children
- Guidelines for good family meetings
- How to get kids to work
- Cleaning tips that make life easier
- How to handle the child's own room
- Cleaning games to make work fun
- The pay-for-work vs. allowance debate

Complete with a discussion guide, *Children Who Do Too Little* is a book every parent will benefit from—and every child as well!

Softcover: 0-310-21146-8

Pick up a copy at your favorite bookstore!

GRAND RAPIDS, MICHIGAN 49530 USA

WWW.ZONDERVAN.COM

When Did We Lose Harriet?

MacLaren Yarbrough Mysteries

Patricia Sprinkle

A teenage girl has been missing from her Montgomery, Alabama, home for six weeks. She may be a runaway, a crime victim, or both. What's amazing is other people's lack of concern. Just one person cares that she's gone—a spunky amateur sleuth on the sunset end of sixty.

Armed with razor-sharp insight, a salty wit, and tenacious faith, MacLaren Yarbrough follows a trail of clues—a wisp of a hint, a shadow of a lie—in search of answers to questions that come hot and fast and that grow increasingly alarming. How did a fifteen-year-old girl come across a large sum of money? Why did she hide it instead of taking it with her? Where is she now? And who is willing to kill to keep MacLaren from probing too far?

Masked by Dixie charm and the scent of honeysuckle, a deadly secret lies coiled—one that holds the ultimate answer to the question, When did we lose Harriet? *When Did We Lose Harriet?* is the first of the MacLaren Yarbrough Mysteries, featuring plucky, sixty-some heroine MacLaren Yarbrough.

Softcover: 0-310-21294-4

But Why Shoot the Magistrate?

MacLaren Yarbrough Mysteries

Patricia Sprinkle

When a popular youth pastor is accused of a grisly crime, MacLaren Yarbrough won't rest until she finds the truth. Her gut instinct tells her Luke Blessed is innocent. Still, how could the dream he had on the night a young woman was murdered depict the crime with such chilling accuracy?

As MacLaren tracks down clues from all corners of Hopewell, Georgia, four likely suspects emerge. But the police aren't buying her theories. Even her husband, local magistrate Joe Riddley, resists her amateur sleuthing. This case, he feels, is too dangerous. Just how dangerous, both of them are about to discover. The assailant strikes again, leaving Joe comatose from a gunshot wound to the head. And suddenly, a new question stares MacLaren in the face. It's the most perplexing question of all—and the most personal: Why shoot the magistrate?

Softcover: 0-310-21324-X

Pick up a copy at your favorite bookstore!

GRAND RAPIDS, MICHIGAN 49530 USA

WWW.ZONDERVAN.COM

The Remember Box

Patricia Sprinkle

I stroked the satin wood in delight and confusion. Why should Uncle Stephen send it to me? The Remember Box was Aunt Kate's private place, the one we were sternly forbidden to open. Suddenly I was reluctant, even fearful—a modern Pandora, about to let out our own lost world. That box held one year I'd spent a lifetime trying to forget.

Summer in Job's Corner meant big trees, cool grass, and sweltering afternoons stretching endlessly under the Southern sun. Those were the days without plastic, microwaves, television, or air conditioning, a time when clocks ticked comfortingly in the night and a cool breeze was a gift. But as the long sultry summer of 1949 comes to an end, events will transform this sleepy Southern crossroads.

After losing her mother to polio, eleven-year-old Carley Marshall comes to Job's Corner to make a new start, along with her Aunt Kate and Uncle Stephen Whitfield and her cousins Abby and John. The family is welcomed warmly by this small North Carolina community as Stephen takes up the post of pastor to Bethel Church, a Presbyterian congregation. But their welcome begins to wear thin and covert criticism runs rampant as Stephen challenges age-old beliefs and traditions.

With the dawning of a new decade, Carley learns to face her own family secrets. And discovers that we all must make the journey to truth alone.

Softcover: 0-310-22992-8

Pick up a copy at your favorite bookstore!

In this exciting sequel to
The Remember Box, a young girl
uncovers more and more secrets in
every corner of her town

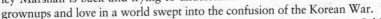

Carley's Song

Patricia Sprinkle

Readers of *The Remember Box* fell in love with the Southern warmth and drama of life in Job's Corner. Now, in *Carley's Song,* the second of the Job's Corner Chronicles, young Carley Marshall is back and trying to understand grownups and love in a world swept into the confusion of the Korean War.

In the fall of 1950 when Carley is twelve, three natives return to Job's Corner after long absences. Clay Lamont, fresh from the Air Force, breaks Carley's heart in her first crush. Maddie Raeburn, beautiful enough to be a movie star, causes quite a stir when she announces she is now divorced and plans to teach seventh grade. And Jerry Donaldson returns to become the school principal, igniting an old grudge in Maddie Raeburn.

Meanwhile, Carley stumbles her way into one secret after another and even comes across an old skull. She begins to wonder what other secrets are hiding in Job's Corner. Will her friends ever find true love? And will she ever come to understand the secretive and often conflicting world of grownups?

Softcover: 0-310-22993-6

Pick up a copy at your favorite bookstore!

GRAND RAPIDS, MICHIGAN 49530 USA

WWW.ZONDERVAN.COM